Jim

With Best Wishes for
your travels in Sabah.

Clive + Ignatia

POCKET GUIDE TO
THE BIRDS OF BORNEO

compiled by

Charles M. Francis
from 3rd. edition by
Bertram E. Smythies
and using the original plates by
Commander A.M. Hughes

The Sabah Society
with
World Wildlife Fund Malaysia
1984

The Sabah Society
P O Box 547
Kota Kinabalu, Sabah

World Wildlife Fund Malaysia
P O Box 10769
Kuala Lumpur

First published 1984

ISBN. 967 — 99947-0-8

Printed in Malaysia
By Pencetak Weng Fatt Sdn Bhd
Lot 8243 Jalan 225, Section 51A, Petaling Jaya, Selangor, Malaysia.

POCKET GUIDE TO THE BIRDS OF BORNEO
INTRODUCTION

The Birds of Borneo by B.E. Smythies is, at present, the only comprehensive guide to Bornean birds. It has the disadvantage, however, that it is a hefty volume, even in the reduced size of the third edition, making it difficult and awkward to use in the field. Many bird observers desire a smaller work that can be easily carried, enabling quick identification of birds as they are seen. In addition, many tourists and visitors are interested in a book which shows the diversity and richness of the Bornean avifauna without being expensive or heavy to pack.

This pocket guide has been prepared in an attempt to fill this need. It is essentially a reduced version of the original work by Smythies comprising the original plates painted by Commander A.M. Hughes, together with any extra information useful to help identify each bird species. Captions are placed opposite the plates (with additional pages where required) giving the common name, scientific name and total length of each species with brief descriptive notes if necessary. Descriptions of species which are not illustrated are placed as close as possible to the captions for related species — these can be distinguished by the absence of a reference number to an illustration.

Most of the information has been condensed from the third edition of *The Birds of Borneo* (1981, Sabah Society & Malay Nature Society), although some additional material has been drawn from other published sources, particularly *A Field Guide to the Birds of South-east Asia* (King, B.F., Dickinson, E.C., & Woodcock, M.W. 1975. Collins: London). Common names from the field guide are given in parentheses whenever they differ from the third edition.

The descriptive notes are designed primarily to highlight the key identification features of hard to identify species and to give some idea of the appearance of unillustrated species. For difficult groups such as waders or birds of prey which are only partly illustrated, the serious ornithologist may have to consult other publications to confirm his identifications. A few blank pages are provided for writing field notes, or adding extra notes on the appearance of species.

Habitat preferences are only indicated in a few cases where they help to separate similar species, but the status is shown for all species which are not permanent residents in Borneo. "Migrant" is used for both passage migrants which stop over in autumn and spring and winter visitors which remain in Borneo for the winter but breed further north. "Visitor" refers to birds which are seen irregularly in Borneo, but breed elsewhere. Abundance is not generally indicated, as many species are common in some areas but uncommon in others. However, a few species known from only a few specimens, often of uncertain status are indicated as "Rare", while birds common elsewhere but which only occasionally stray to Borneo on migration are marked as "Vagrant". For the benefit of foreign visitors species known only from Borneo are marked with an asterisk ('*').

Charles M. Francis   July 1984

ACKNOWLEDGEMENTS

This volume contains the original plates painted by Commander A.M. Hughes using new transparencies and colour separations giving a more faithful representation of the originals. We are indeed very grateful to Lady Y.P. McNeice for allowing us access to and use of her folio and to Mr Ken Scriven of the World Wildlife Fund Malaysia for making all the arrangements. The publishers also wish to thank Mr Charles Francis for his work in preparing the text.

CONTENTS

PLATE A
BOOBIES, Grebe and Petrels

1. MASKED BOOBY, *Sula dactylatra.* 1) Adult, 1a) Immature. 34" (84cm). Rare visitor.

2. RED-FOOTED BOOBY, *Sula sula.* 2) Adult, 2a) Immature. 28" (70cm). Adult from Masked Booby by white tail. Immature: head often brown but never darker than belly. Visitor.

3. BROWN BOOBY, *Sula leucogaster.* 3) Adult, 3a) Immature. 29" (75cm). Immature: dark brown head and breast sharply cut off from paler belly.

   LITTLE GREBE or DABCHICK, *Podiceps ruficollis.* 10" (25cm). A small brown diving bird with a short bill. Streams and ponds. Vagrant.

   SWINHOE'S STORM-PETREL, *Oceanodroma monorhis.* 6" (15cm). Dark brown with forked tail; fluttery flight. Oceanic vagrant.

   BULWER'S PETREL, *Bulweria bulwerii.* 10½" (27cm). All dark brown with pale band on greater wing coverts; wedge-shaped tail; fluttery, erratic flight. Oceanic visitor.

   STREAKED SHEARWATER, *Calonectris leucomelas.* 19" (48cm). Brown back; white underparts; pale head with thin streaks. Oceanic migrant.

PLATE A

1

1a

2

2a

3

3a

0"   6"   12"   18"   24"

0   200   mm   400   600

R. Hughes 1958.

PLATE B
FRIGATEBIRDS

1. CHRISTMAS FRIGATEBIRD, *Fregata andrewsi*. 1) Male, 1a) Female, 1b) Immature. 37'' (95cm). White lower belly distinctive in adult. Immatures of all three frigatebirds are hard to distinguish.

2. LESSER FRIGATEBIRD, *Fregata ariel*. 2) Male, 2a) Female, 2b) Immature. 32'' (80cm). Female from Great Frigatebird Female by black instead of greyish throat.

3. GREAT FRIGATEBIRD, *Fregata minor*. 3) Male, 3a) Female, 3b) Immature. 37'' (95cm).

1   1a   1b

2   2a   2b

3   3a   3b

0" 6" 12" 18" 24" 30" 36" 42" 48"
0 200 400 600 800 1000 1200
mm

A. Hughes
1958.

PLATE I
CORMORANTS, DARTERS, HERONS AND STORKS
Ibises and Spoonbill

1. ORIENTAL DARTER, *Anhinga melanogaster.* 36" (90cm).

2. COMMON (GREAT) CORMORANT, *Phalacrocorax carbo.* 35" (88cm). Head dark in winter.

   LITTLE BLACK CORMORANT, *Phalacrocorax sulcirostris.* 25" (63cm). Small and black. Immature all dark brown. Rare.

   LITTLE CORMORANT, *Phalacrocorax niger.* 22" (55cm). Small and black; whitish throat in winter. Shorter bill and wing than Little Black Cormorant. Rare.

3. DUSKY-GREY (GREAT-BILLED) HERON, *Ardea sumatrana.* 45" (110cm).

4. PURPLE HERON, *Ardea purpurea.* 38" (96cm).

5. GREY HERON, *Ardea cinerea.* 40" (100cm).

6. STORM'S STORK. *Ciconia stormi.* 34" (85cm).

   LESSER ADJUTANT, *Leptoptilos javanicus.* 45" (110cm). Large stork with naked head and neck, all white underparts, dark upperparts and wings.

7. RUFOUS NIGHT-HERON, *Nycticorax caledonicus.* 25" (63cm). Immature: pale grey-brown with whitish streaks; cinnamon wash on wings and tail.

8. COMMON (BLACK-CROWNED) NIGHT-HERON, *Nycticorax nycticorax.* 24" (61cm). Immature dull brown with buff spots above, pale with brown streaks below.

   BLACK-HEADED IBIS *Threskiornis melanocephalus.* 25" (63cm). White plumage with black head and neck, long decurved bill. Rare migrant.

   GLOSSY IBIS, *Plegadis falcinellus.* 24" (61cm). All dark plumage, long decurved bill. Vagrant.

   BLACK IBIS, *Pseudibis papillosa.* 30" (75cm). All black, with bare head, and conspicuous white wing spot. Rare.

   WHITE SPOONBILL, *Platalea leucorodia.* 33" (84cm). All white with spoon-shaped bill. Migrant.

PLATE I

PLATE II
EGRETS, BITTERNS AND HERONS

1. INTERMEDIATE (PLUMED) EGRET, *Egretta intermedia.* 28''
   (71cm). Legs and feet black. Winter: bill yellow. Breeding: bill
   black, long plumes on breast and back. Migrant.

2. CHINESE EGRET, *Egretta eulophotes.* 27'' (69cm). Winter: legs
   yellowish; bill dusky; facial skin greenish. Breeding: legs black with
   yellowish feet; bill yellow; facial skin dark blue; plumes on lower
   back; shaggy crest. Migrant.

3. (PACIFIC) REEF EGRET, *Egretta sacra.* 23'' (58cm). a) White
   Phase, b) Dark Phase. White phase from other egrets by greenish
   legs, dusky yellow bill. Sandy or rocky shores.

   LARGE (GREAT) EGRET, *Egretta alba.* 35'' (89cm). Like
   Intermediate Egret but larger, more massive bill, neck more kinked.
   Breeding: legs reddish; plumes on lower back only. Migrant.

   LITTLE EGRET, *Egretta garzetta.* 24'' (61cm). Legs black with
   yellow feet; bill black with yellow base. Breeding: crest of two long
   narrow plumes. Migrant.

   CATTLE EGRET, *Bubulcus ibis.* 20'' (51cm). Legs and bill yellow;
   thick, relatively short bill; puffed throat. Breeding: buff head and
   neck. Migrant.

4. LITTLE GREEN (LITTLE) HERON, *Butorides striatus.* 16''
   (40cm).

5. YELLOW BITTERN, *Ixobrychus sinensis.* 14'' (36cm). Black
   primaries contrast with buffy wing coverts. Migrant.

6. CINNAMON BITTERN, *Ixobrychus cinnamomeus.* 15'' (38cm).
   Uniform rufous wings.

7. CHINESE POND-HERON, *Ardeola bacchus.* 18'' (46cm). Wings
   are pure white. Migrant.

   JAVAN POND-HERON, *Ardeola speciosa.* 18'' (46cm). Like
   Chinese Pond Heron, but in breeding plumage, head and neck
   brownish buff, breast cinnamon. Both species are streaky brown in
   winter. Migrant.

8. TIGER BITTERN (MALAYSIAN NIGHT-HERON), *Gorsachius
   melanolophus.* 19'' (48cm). Black primaries with white tips.
   Immature: similar but browner, white spots on crown, buff stripe on
   back. Migrant.

9. BLACK BITTERN, *Dupetor flavicollis.* 23'' (58cm). Migrant.

10. SCHRENCK'S BITTERN, *Ixobrychus eurhythmus.* 14'' (36cm).
    Flight pattern like Yellow Bittern, but coverts contrast less with
    flight feathers, upperparts dark chestnut (flecked white in
    female). Migrant.

PLATE II

Am Hughes
1955

Ducks

INDIAN WHISTLING DUCK (LESSER TREEDUCK), *Dendrocygna javanica.* 16" (41cm). Long-legged duck with long neck, rufous plumage, buffy brown head.

WANDERING WHISTLING DUCK, *Dendrocygna arcuata.* 17" (43cm). Like Indian Whistling Duck, but with black and white markings on flanks. Rare.

MALLARD, *Anas platyrhynchos.* 23" (58cm). Base stock of domestic duck. Purplish speculum with white borders. Male: green head, grey and black body. Female: brown. Migrant.

(EURASIAN) WIGEON, *Anas penelope.* 19" (48cm). Short bill; rounded head; white patch on front of wing contrasts with dark flight feathers. Male: chestnut head with buffy crown; white patch on brown flanks. Female: uniform rufous brown all over. Migrant.

COMMON PINTAIL, *Anas acuta.* 22" (55cm). Slender body; long neck and tail. Male: chocolate brown head and neck with white stripe; grey body. Female: mottled brown with whitish belly; white trailing edge to brown wing.

GARGANEY, *Anas querquedula.* 16" (41cm). Male: brown head with broad white eyebrow; dark plumage. Female: mottled dull brown with whitish eyebrow and white lower cheeks.

(NORTHERN) SHOVELER, *Anas clypeata.* 20" (50cm). Long broad bill; pale wing coverts contrast with dark flight feathers. Male: white breast and sides, green head and chestnut belly. Female: mottled brown with dark eye stripe.

TUFTED DUCK, *Aythya fuligula.* 17" (43cm). Broad white wing bar in flight. Male: glossy black with white belly and flanks; black crest. Female: black replaced by dark brown.

COTTON TEAL (PYGMY GOOSE), *Nettapus coromandelianus.* 13" (33cm). Male: all white except black crown, collar and back. Female: similar, but black replaced by brown, white tinged buffy.

NOTES

PLATE III
BIRDS OF PREY

WHITE-RUMPED VULTURE, *Gyps bengalensis*. 35'' (90cm). Large heavily built raptor with blackish plumage; white rump and lower back; whitish wing lining. Vagrant.

BLACK-SHOULDERED KITE, *Elanus caeruleus*. 13'' (33cm). Pearly grey upperparts with large black shoulder patches; white underparts. Often hovers.

1. **BAT HAWK**, *Machaeramphus alcinus*. 18'' (46cm). Falcon-like in flight but with broader wings.

2. **JERDON'S BAZA**, *Aviceda jerdoni*. 16-19'' (40-48cm). Long wings reach nearly to tip of tail; white tips to black crest.

3. **BRAHMINY KITE**, *Haliastur indus*. 18'' (46cm). Immature mottled brown; wings pale at base, blackish on outer ⅔.

 BLACK KITE, *Milvus migrans*. 28'' (71cm). Dark brown with long angled wings and long forked tail. Vagrant.

4. **CRESTED GOSHAWK**, *Accipiter trivirgatus*. 14'' (36cm). Accipiters have short round wings and longish tails. This is the only crested species.

 JAPANESE SPARROWHAWK, *Accipiter gularis*. MALE 10'' (25cm). FEMALE 12'' (30cm). Dark slaty upperparts with blackish crown; breast and belly pale rufous with some white bars; streaked throat. Immature: dark brown above, streaked brown below. Migrant.

 CHINESE GOSHAWK, *Accipiter soloensis*. 11'' (28cm). Adult: Like Japanese Sparrowhawk, but white underside of secondaries contrasts with black outer primaries. Migrant.

 BESRA, *Accipiter virgatus*. 10-13'' (25-33cm). Like Japanese Sparrowhawk, but broad dark mesial stripe on white throat. Montane.

 NORTHERN SPARROWHAWK, *Accipiter nisus*. 14'' (36cm). Larger than Japanese Sparrowhawk with almost unstreaked throat. Vagrant.

5. **BLYTH'S HAWK-EAGLE**, *Spizaetus alboniger*. 20-21'' (50-53cm). Immature has black replaced by brown, underparts streaked.

 WALLACE'S HAWK-EAGLE, *Spizaetus nanus*. 17-19'' (43-48cm). Similar to Blyth's Hawk-Eagle, but smaller, browner; tail has two or three white bands.

Continued on next page.

PLATE III

CHANGEABLE HAWK-EAGLE, *Spizaetus cirrhatus*. 26" (66cm). Dark phase: Like Black Eagle, but underside of primaries paler than wing lining; pale base to tail. Light phase: dark brown upperparts; streaked breast; slight crest.

RUFOUS-BELLIED EAGLE, *Hieraaetus kienerii*. 18" (45cm). Black crown and cheeks; whitish throat; rufous belly and underwing; dark grey upperparts; white bases to primaries. Immature: whitish underneath with pale head.

6. GREY-FACED BUZZARD, *Butastur indicus*. 17" (43cm). Very long wings; contrasting rufous breast and greyish head; some white on upper tail coverts. Immature: whitish breast with broad brown streaks. Migrant.

7. LESSER FISH-EAGLE, *Ichthyophaga nana*. 19" (48cm). Immature browner.

GREY-HEADED FISH-EAGLE, *Ichthyophaga ichthyaetus*. 26" (66cm). Like Lesser Fish-eagle, but larger; basal ⅔ of tail white (conspicuous from above).

WHITE-BELLIED SEA-EAGLE, *Haliaeetus leucogaster*. 26" (66cm). White belly, head and wing lining; blackish flight feathers; grey upperparts; wedge-shaped tail. Immature dark brown with buff head and belly.

8. CRESTED SERPENT-EAGLE. *Spilornis cheela*. 19" (48cm). Adult: Broad white band across middle of flight feathers. Immature: dark brown above; whitish below with some streaking.

 * MOUNTAIN SERPENT-EAGLE, *Spilornis kinabaluensis*. 22" (55cm). Like Crested Serpent-Eagle, but underparts darker, throat black.

9. CRESTED HONEY-BUZZARD, *Pernis ptilorhynchus*. 22" (55cm). Variable plumage. Two dark bands at base of tail and one near tip; Protruding pigeon-like head.

10. BLACK EAGLE, *Ictinaetus malayensis*. 27" (68cm). From Changeable Hawk-Eagle by uniform dark underparts; faint pale barring on tail. Immature: paler above, underparts tawny brown with heavy streaking.

MARSH HARRIER, *Circus aeruginosus*. 20" (50cm). Harriers have long tails and long wings which they hold in a V-shape as they fly low over open areas. Marsh Harrier has heavier build than other harriers. Male like Pied Harrier male, but throat streaked black and white; immature: body streaked dark brown. Female dark brown with pale cream throat and forewing; dark rump.

PIED HARRIER, *Circus melanoleucos*. 17'' (43cm). Adult male pale grey with black head and back; black wing tips and carpal bar. Female uniform streaked brown upperparts; buffy underparts; white rump. Immature dark brown above; chestnut below; white rump.

HEN (NORTHERN) HARRIER, *Circus cyaneus*. 18'' (46cm). Adult male grey above with black wing tips and white rump; white below. Female and immature very like Pied Harrier female.

OSPREY, *Pandion haliaetus*. 20-23'' (50-58cm). White head and underparts; brown upperparts; dark brown stripe from eye to nape; brown breast band; dark carpal patches and wing tips.

BLACK-THIGHED FALCONET, *Microhierax fringillarius*. 6'' (15cm). Tiny falcon with black crown and band through eye; white forehead, cheeks, eyebrow and breast; black upperparts; rufous belly; black thighs. S. Borneo and Sarawak.

* **WHITE-FRONTED FALCONET**, *Microhierax latifrons*. 6'' (15cm). Like Black-thighed Falconet, but front half of head white, underparts buffy. N. Borneo only.

PEREGRINE FALCON, *Falco peregrinus*. 14-19'' (35-48cm). Slaty grey upperparts; black head with dark moustache; white throat; dark barred underparts. Immature dark brown with streaks below.

ORIENTAL HOBBY, *Falco severus*. 10'' (25cm). Grey head and upperparts; no moustachial stripe; dark chestnut underparts. Vagrant.

(EURASIAN) KESTREL, *Falco tinnunculus*. 13-14'' (33-35cm). Banded rufous upperparts; lightly streaked underparts; tail grey (male), or rufous (female). Rare Migrant.

SPOTTED KESTREL, *Falco moluccensis*. 13-14'' (33-35cm). Like Kestrel, but yellowish-red spotted and streaked with black; grey rump and tail with black bars. Vagrant.

PLATE IV
MEGAPODE, PARTRIDGES AND PHEASANTS

1. MEGAPODE, *Megapodius freycinet.* 14'' (36cm).

2. LONG-BILLED PARTRIDGE, *Rhizothera longirostris.* 12'' (30cm). S. Borneo and Sarawak only.

3.* RED-BREASTED PARTRIDGE, *Arborophila hyperythra.* 11'' (27cm). Montane.

4. FERRUGINOUS WOOD PARTRIDGE, *Caloperdix oculea.* 9'' (23cm). Montane.

5. BLACK WOOD PARTRIDGE, *Melanoperdix nigra.* a) Male, b) Female. 10'' (25cm). Lowlands in S. and W. Borneo.

6. SCALY-BREASTED PARTRIDGE, *Arborophila charltoni.* 11'' (28cm). Sabah.

7. CRESTLESS FIREBACK, *Lophura erthrophthalma.* a) Male, b) Female. 19'' (48cm). S. and W. Borneo.

8. CRESTED FIREBACK, *Lophura ignita.* a) Male, b) Female 22'' (55cm).

PLATE IV

1

2

3

4

5b

5a

6

7b

7a

8b

8a

Anthughes
1955

0"   6"   12"
0   100   mm   200   300

PLATE V
PARTRIDGES AND BULWER'S PHEASANT

CRESTED WOOD PARTRIDGE, *Rollulus rouloul.* (Bottom left). Male left, Female right. 10" (25cm).

* CRIMSON-HEADED PARTRIDGE, *Haematortyx sanguiniceps.* (Bottom right). Male right, Female left. 10" (25cm). Montane.

* BULWER'S PHEASANT, *Lophura bulweri.* (Top). Male (right) 31" (88cm), Female (left) 20" (50cm).

PLATE VI
PHEASANTS

1. MALAYSIAN PEACOCK-PHEASANT, *Polyplectron malacense.* (bottom). Male (left) 17'' (43cm), Female (right) 15'' (38cm).

2. GREAT ARGUS, *Argusianus argus,* (top). Male (left) 66'' (170cm). Female (right) 24'' (61cm).

PLATE VII
QUAIL, CRAKES and Jacanas

1. BLUE-BREASTED QUAIL, *Coturnix chinensis.* a) Male, b) Female. 5'' (13cm).

2. SLATY-BREASTED RAIL, *Rallus striatus.* 9'' (23cm). Chestnut crown.

   WATER RAIL, *Rallus aquaticus.* 10'' (25cm). Like Slaty-breasted Rail, but upperparts including crown dark brown streaked with black; longer bill. Vagrant.

3. BAND-BELLIED CRAKE, *Porzana paykulli.* 8'' (20cm). From Red-legged Crake by unbarred flight feathers; olive-brown crown and hindneck. Migrant.

4. BAILLON'S CRAKE, *Porzana pusilla.* 6'' (15cm). Rare.

5. RUDDY-BREASTED CRAKE, *Porzana fusca.* 7'' (18cm). No white in wings; inconspicuous white barring under tail. Rare.

6. RED-LEGGED CRAKE, *Rallina fasciata.* 8'' (20cm). White barring on flight feathers; broad black and white barring under tail.

7. WHITE-BROWED CRAKE, *Porzana cinerea.* 7'' (18cm).

8. WHITE-BREASTED WATERHEN, *Amaurornis phoenicurus.* 10'' (25cm).

9. WATERCOCK, *Gallicrex cinerea* (Winter). 13'' (33cm). Adult male black; red bill and frontal shield; red legs. Migrant.

   PURPLE SWAMPHEN, *Porphyrio porphyrio.* 13'' (33cm). Purple and blue plumage; red legs; thick red bill.

   COMMON MOORHEN, *Gallinula chloropus.* 12'' (30cm). Black plumage; red and yellow bill; white undertail coverts; white spots on flanks; greenish legs.

   BLACK MOORHEN, *Gallinula tenebrosa.* 12'' (30cm). Like Common Moorhen, but no white on flanks; reddish legs. S. Borneo only.

   COOT, *Fulica atra.* 15'' (38cm). Slaty black; white bill and frontal shield. Rare migrant.

   PHEASANT-TAILED JACANA, *Hydrophasianus chirurgus.* 12'' (30cm); tail up to 10'' (25cm) longer. Long legs and toes; slender white neck with yellow nape. Breeding: white wings; dark brown body; long brown tail. Non-breeding: pale brown body and chest; white belly. S. Borneo only.

   COMB-CRESTED JACANA, *Irediparra gallinacea.* 10'' (25cm). Brownish above with black markings; white throat with orange border; black breastband; white belly; red wattle on forehead. S. Borneo only.

PLATE VII

PLATE C
WADERS

1. **GREY PLOVER**, *Pluvialis squatarola*. 11" (26cm). Mottled greyish upperparts; whitish tail and wing bar; black axillaries on white underwing. Black belly in summer. Migrant.

2. **LESSER GOLDEN PLOVER**, *Pluvialis dominica*. 10" (25cm). Upperparts mottled dark brown and buff. Winter: underparts buffy. Breeding: underparts black. Migrant.

   GREY-HEADED LAPWING, *Vanellus cinereus*. 14" (36cm). Grey back, head and upper breast; black band on lower breast; black primaries; white secondaries; white tail with black subterminal band. Vagrant.

3. **MALAYSIAN PLOVER**, *Charadrius peronii*. 6" (15cm). Sandy upperparts with buffy scales; white wing bar. Male: broad black band across upper back; separate black loral and ear patches. Female: black replaced by sandy rufous.

   KENTISH PLOVER, *Charadrius alexandrinus*. 6" (15cm). Like Malaysian Plover, but plain brown upperparts; no black band on back; black mark on face stretches through eye. Migrant.

   LITTLE RINGED PLOVER, *Charadrius dubius*. 7" (18cm). Like Malaysian Plover, but complete black breast band in adult (brown in immature); no white wing bar. Migrant.

4. **GREATER SAND-PLOVER**, *Charadrius leschenaultii*. 9" (23cm). Grey-brown upperparts; whitish underparts; grey patches on side of breast; white wingbar; bill over 21mm. Breeding: rufous breast band. Migrant.

   MONGOLIAN PLOVER, *Charadrius mongolus*. 8" (20cm). Very like Greater Sand-Plover, but smaller: bill less than 21mm. Migrant.

5. **ORIENTAL PLOVER**, *Charadrius veredus*. 9" (23cm). Like Lesser Golden Plover in stance but smaller; upperparts plain brown; broad grey-brown (winter) or chestnut (breeding) breast band. Faint wing bar. Migrant.

6. **(COMMON) REDSHANK**, *Tringa totanus*. 11" (28cm). Mottled brown upperparts; broad white trailing edge to wing; white wedge up middle of back; red or orange legs. Migrant.

   SPOTTED REDSHANK, *Tringa erythropus*. 12" (30cm). Like Common Redshank, but narrower black bill; no white in wings; paler and greyer. Breeding: black with white spots. Migrant.

Continued on next page.

PLATE C

Am Hughes
1958

(COMMON) GREENSHANK, *Tringa nebularia.* 14'' (35cm). Like winter Spotted Redshank, but pale greenish legs; stout slightly upturned bill with pale base; darker grey upperparts. Migrant.

NORDMANN'S GREENSHANK, *Tringa guttifer.* 13'' (33cm). Very like Common Greenshank, but stouter bill with yellow base and black tip; shorter and yellower legs. Rare migrant.

MARSH SANDPIPER, *Tringa stagnatilis.* 10'' (25cm). Like Common Greenshank, but smaller, slighter build; narrow black bill. Migrant.

7. BAR-TAILED GODWIT, *Limosa lapponica.* 15'' (38cm). White rump and tail with fine black bars; mottled greyish brown upperparts; long slightly upcurved bill; no wing bar. Breeding: Mottled black and brown above; rufous below. Migrant.

BLACK-TAILED GODWIT, *Limosa limosa.* 16'' (40cm). Like Bar-tailed Godwit, but broad white wing bar; tail white with broad black band at tip; upperparts greyer and less mottled. Migrant.

ASIATIC (ASIAN) DOWITCHER, *Limnodromus semipalmatus.* 14'' (36cm). Like Bar-tailed Godwit, but bill straight, all black, thickened at tip. Migrant.

8. WHIMBREL, *Numenius phaeopus.* 17'' (43cm). Whitish rump and tail; buff and dark brown stripes on crown; bill 7-10cm. Migrant.

LITTLE CURLEW, *Numenius minutus.* 12'' (30cm). Like a miniature Whimbrel with a shorter bill (5cm). Migrant.

9. GREAT THICK-KNEE, *Esacus magnirostris.* 20'' (50cm).

10. LONG-BILLED (EASTERN) CURLEW, *Numenius madagascariensis.* 23'' (58cm). Larger than Whimbrel with longer bill (17-18cm); uniform brown upperparts including rump and tail. Migrant.

COMMON (EURASIAN) CURLEW, *Numenius arquata.* 23'' (58cm). Like Long-billed Curlew, but rump white; bill shorter (12-15cm). Migrant.

BLACK-WINGED STILT, *Himantopus himantopus.* 15'' (38cm). White head and body; black wings; long thin black bill; very long pink legs. Migrant.

NOTES

PLATE D
WADERS

1. **WOOD SANDPIPER,** *Tringa glareola*. 9'' (23cm). Mottled brown body and rump; white tail and upper tail coverts; pale underwing; no wing bar; pale eyestripe and eyering. Migrant.

   GREEN SANDPIPER, *Tringa ochropus*. 9½'' (24cm). Like Wood Sandpiper, but darker upperparts; blackish underwing; eyestripe, but no eyering. Migrant.

2. **COMMON SANDPIPER,** *Actitis hypoleucos*. 8'' (20cm). Brown patch on side of breast; white wing stripe; dark tail with white outer feathers; teetering walk and stiff-winged flight. Migrant.

3. **TEREK SANDPIPER,** *Xenus cinereus*. 9'' (23cm). Long upturned bill; short orange-yellow legs; white trailing edge to wing. Migrant.

4. **GREY-TAILED TATTLER,** *Heteroscelus brevipes*. 10'' (25cm). Unmarked dark grey upperparts; straight dark bill; pale grey or finely barred underparts. Migrant.

5. **(RUDDY) TURNSTONE,** *Arenaria interpres*. 9'' (23cm). Distinct dark and white pattern on wings and tail; dark breast patch; orange legs. Breeding: rufous orange above. Migrant.

6. **SNIPES.** These are distinguished by long bills, stripes on the crown, mottled pattern on back and habit of rising suddenly from dense cover. The three species are mainly separated by wing and tail pattern:

A. **PINTAIL SNIPE,** *Gallinago stenura*. 11'' (28cm). Very narrow outer tail feathers (1mm at tip); dark trailing edge to wing. Migrant.

B. **FANTAIL (COMMON) SNIPE,** *Gallinago gallinago*. 11'' (28cm). 12-18 fairly broad tail feathers; narrow white band on trailing edge of secondaries. Migrant.

C. **SWINHOE'S SNIPE,** *Gallinago megala*. 11'' (28cm). 20 tail feathers, outer ones 2-3mm at tip; dark trailing edge to wing. Migrant.

   (GREATER) PAINTED SNIPE, *Rostratula benghalensis*. 10'' (25cm). Shaped like a snipe, though unrelated. Buff crown stripe; white eyering and eyestripe; buff spotted wings. Migrant.

7. **GREAT KNOT,** *Calidris tenuirostris*. 12'' (30cm). Stout and greyish; dark spots on breast and flanks; indistinct wing bar; white upper tail coverts contrast with dark tail. Migrant.

   COMMON (RED) KNOT, *Calidris canutus*. 10'' (25cm). Like Great Knot, but smaller with shorter bill; light streaks on underparts; little contrast between whitish coverts and tail. Breeding: all orange red. Migrant.

Continued on next page.

A. Hughes

0" 3" 6"
0   50   mm   100   150

SANDERLING, *Crocethia alba.* 8'' (20cm). Broad white wing bar in flight; pearly grey upperparts; white underparts; dark shoulder patch. Breeding: Head, breast and upperparts mottled rufous and black. Migrant.

8. RUFOUS-NECKED STINT, *Calidris ruficollis.* 6½'' (16cm). Small size and short bill; whitish wing bar; dark centre of tail and rump, pale grey outer tail feathers; indistinctly streaked grey upperparts; dark legs. Migrant.

LONG-TOED STINT, *Calidris subminuta.* 6'' (15cm). Like Rufous-necked Stint, but browner upperparts with bold black streaks; yellowish or greenish legs. Migrant.

TEMMINCK'S STINT, *Calidris temminckii.* 6'' (15cm). Like Rufous-necked Stint, but darker and duller brownish grey upperparts; pure white outer tail feathers; yellowish or greenish legs. Migrant.

SHARP-TAILED SANDPIPER, *Calidris acuminata.* 8½'' (22cm). Like a large Long-toed Stint with streaked rufous cap; buffy breast with variable streaking. Migrant.

CURLEW SANDPIPER, *Calidris ferruginea.* 8½'' (22cm). Decurved black bill; white rump; greyish upperparts; white wing bar, eyebrow and underparts. Breeding: mottled rufous and black above, orange below. Migrant.

BROAD-BILLED SANDPIPER, *Limicola falcinellus.* 7'' (18cm). Like a small Curlew Sandpiper, but bill flattened and broadened; double white eyebrow; dark centre of rump. Summer: rufous and blackish upperparts; streaked brown breast. Migrant.

RUFF and REEVE, *Philomachus pugnax.* Male 12'' (30cm). Female 10'' (25cm). Narrow neck and short bill; dark brown upperparts with buffy brown scaling; narrow white wing bar; oval white patches on sides of dark tail. Migrant.

RED-NECKED PHALAROPE, *Phalaropus lobatus.* 7½'' (19cm). Streaked dark grey upperparts; white underparts; black patch through eye; broad white wingstripe; narrow black bill. Breeding: rufous breast and sides of neck. Migrant.

GREY (RED) PHALAROPE, *Phalaropus fulicarius.* 8'' (20cm). Like Red-necked Phalarope but thicker bill with yellowish base; paler grey upperparts with no streaks; whiter crown. Breeding: chestnut plumage with white sides to head. Rare Migrant.

9. ORIENTAL PRATINCOLE, *Glareola maldivarum.* 10'' (25cm). Brown upperparts; forked tail; tern-like flight; rufous underwings.

LONG-LEGGED PRATINCOLE, *Glareola isabella.* 10'' (25cm). Like Oriental Pratincole, but legs longer; lacks black throat border; deep chestnut flanks. Rare Migrant.

NOTES

PLATE VIII
GULL, TERNS, Skuas and Noddies

1. (COMMON) BLACK-HEADED GULL, *Larus ridibundus.* (Winter). 16'' (41cm). White wedge on leading edge of wing. Breeding: dark brown head. Migrant.

2. WHITE-WINGED BLACK TERN, *Chlidonias leucopterus.* (Winter). 9'' (23cm). Unforked tail; ear patch separate from crown; rump often paler than back. Breeding: black head and body, white wings with black lining. Migrant.

3. WHISKERED TERN, *Chlidonias hybridus.* (Winter). 10'' (25cm). Unforked tail; rump same colour as back; black band from eyes to nape. Breeding: black cap; grey belly; white cheeks. Migrant.

4. BLACK-NAPED TERN, *Sterna sumatrana.* 12'' (30cm). Very white plumage.

5. GULL-BILLED TERN, *Gelochelidon nilotica.* (Winter). 13'' (33cm). Large size; thick bill; shallow fork in tail; dusky patch on ear. Breeding: black cap. Migrant.

6. BRIDLED TERN, *Sterna anaethetus.* 15'' (38cm). Narrow white eyebrow and forehead.

7. LITTLE TERN, *Sterna albifrons.* (Winter). 9'' (23cm). Small size; forked tail. Breeding plumage: black cap; white forehead; yellow bill with black tip.

8. SOOTY TERN, *Sterna fuscata.* 16'' (40cm). Broad white on forehead; short eyebrow; darker back than Bridled Tern. Rare visitor.

9. LESSER CRESTED TERN, *Sterna bengalensis.* (Winter). 15'' (38cm). Narrow orange bill. Breeding: black forehead. Visitor.

10. GREAT CRESTED TERN, *Sterna bergii.* 18'' (46cm). Large, pale yellow bill.

    CHINESE CRESTED TERN, *Sterna zimmermanni.* 17'' (43cm). Very like Lesser Crested Tern, but bill yellow with black tip. Vagrant.

    COMMON TERN, *Sterna hirundo.* 13'' (33cm). Pale grey upperparts, whitish underparts, forked tail with dark outer feathers; black cap. Winter: dark band on leading edge of forewing; white forehead. Migrant.

Continued on next page.

PLATE VIII

ROSEATE TERN, *Sterna dougallii*. 14'' (35cm). Like Common Tern, but whiter above, white outer tail feathers, longer tail.

COMMON (BROWN) NODDY, *Anous stolidus*. 16'' (40cm). All chocolate brown except for pale grey cap; wedge shaped tail; wing > 260mm. Visitor.

WHITE-CAPPED NODDY, *Anous minutus*. 13½'' (34cm). Like Common Noddy, but smaller, (wing < 250mm), more slender bill, blacker plumage, whiter cap. Visitor.

POMARINE SKUA (JAEGAR), *Stercorarius pomarinus*. 20'' (50cm). Dark brown above with white patches at base of primaries; dark brown or white below; projecting central tail feathers thick and twisted. Vagrant.

ARCTIC SKUA (PARASITIC JAEGAR), *Stercorarius parasiticus*. 18'' (46cm). Like Pomarine Skua but smaller; lighter flight; central tail feathers shorter, thin and pointed. Vagrant.

NOTES

PLATE IX
GREEN PIGEONS

1. LARGE GREEN PIGEON, *Treron capelli,* a) Male, b) Female. 14''
   (36cm).

2. THICK-BILLED PIGEON, *Treron curvirostra.* a) Male, b) Female.
   9'' (23cm).

3. CINNAMON-HEADED PIGEON, *Treron fulvicollis.* a) Male,
   b) Female. 10'' (25cm). Female very like Thick-billed Pigeon female
   but undertail coverts streaked not barred.

4. LITTLE GREEN PIGEON, *Treron olax.* a) Male, b) Female. 8½''
   (22cm). No red on bill; broad grey band on tip of tail.

5. PINK-NECKED PIGEON, *Treron vernans.* a) Male, b) Female. 9''
   (23cm). No red on bill; grey tail with broad black subterminal band
   and narrow grey tip.

PLATE IX

1a

1b

2a

2b

3a

3b

4a

4b

5a

5b

0"   3"   6"
0   50   mm 100   150

A. Hughes
1955

PLATE X
DOVES AND PIGEONS

1. JAMBU FRUIT DOVE, *Ptilinopus jambu.* a) Male, b) Female. 10'' (25cm).

2. BLACK-NAPED FRUIT DOVE, *Ptilinopus melanospila.* a) Male, b) Female. 9'' (23cm). Sabah Islands only.

3. GREEN IMPERIAL PIGEON, *Ducula aenea.* 16'' (41cm).

4. GREY IMPERIAL PIGEON, *Ducula pickeringi.* 16'' (41cm). Bronze grey mantle; pale undertail coverts.

5. PIED IMPERIAL PIGEON, *Ducula bicolor.* 14'' (36cm).

6. MOUNTAIN IMPERIAL PIGEON, *Ducula badia.* 17'' (43cm). Usually montane.

7. METALLIC WOOD-PIGEON, *Columba vitiensis.* 16'' (41cm).

8. GREY WOOD-PIGEON, *Columba argentina.* 14'' (36cm). From Pied Imperial Pigeon by greyish plumage, green bill, red eyering.

9. NICOBAR PIGEON, *Caloenas nicobarica.* 14'' (36cm). Islands only.

DOMESTIC PIGEON or ROCK DOVE, *Columba livia,* 13'' (33cm). Originally blue-grey with two black wing bars and a black tail band, but feral stock has many variations including white and brown. Towns and houses. Introduced.

PLATE X

PLATE XI
DOVES

1. **RED CUCKOO-DOVE**, *Macropygia phasianella.* a) Male, b) Female. 12'' (30cm). Male: Plain purplish brown breast and abdomen. Female: heavy black barring on breast. Submontane.

2. **LITTLE CUCKOO-DOVE**, *Macropygia ruficeps.* a) Male, b) Female. 11'' (28cm). From Red Cuckoo-Dove by smaller size, buffy brown breast mottled with black or white spots. Montane.

3. **BARRED GROUND (PEACEFUL) DOVE**, *Geopelia striata.* 7'' (18cm).

4. **JAVANESE TURTLE DOVE**, *Streptopelia bitorquata.* 12'' (30cm). Rare.

5. **SPOTTED DOVE**, *Streptopelia chinensis.* 11'' (28cm).

6. **EMERALD DOVE (GREEN-WINGED PIGEON)**, *Chalcophaps indica.* a) Male, b) Female. 9'' (23cm).

PLATE XI

1a

1b

2a

2b

3

4

5

6a

6b

0"   3"   6"

0   50   mm   100   150

A. Hughes

1956

PLATE XII
PARROTS, BEE-EATERS, ROLLER and Hoopoe

1. LONG-TAILED PARAKEET, *Psittacula longicauda.* 10'' (25cm). Male tail 6'' (15cm) longer.

2. RED-BREASTED PARAKEET, *Psittacula alexandri.* 12'' (30cm). S. Borneo only.

3. MALAY LORIKEET (BLUE-CROWNED HANGING PARROT), *Loriculus galgulus.* a) Male, b) Female. 5'' (13cm).

4. BLUE-NAPED PARROT, *Tanygnathus lucionensis.* 12'' (30cm). Sabah islands only.

5. BLUE-RUMPED PARROT, *Psittinus cyanurus,* a) Male, b) Female. 7'' (18cm). Underwing bright red.

6. BLUE-THROATED BEE-EATER, *Merops viridis.* 11'' (28cm).

7. BLUE-TAILED BEE-EATER, *Merops philippinus.* 12'' (30cm). Migrant.

8. RED-BEARDED BEE-EATER, *Nyctyornis amictus.* 11'' (28cm).

9. BROAD-BILLED ROLLER (DOLLARBIRD), *Eurystomus orientalis.* 11'' (28cm).

    HOOPOE, *Upupa epops.* 12'' (30cm). Pinkish-brown plumage; black wings and tail with white bands; tall crest; long decurved bill. Vagrant.

PLATE XII

A. Hughes
1956

PLATE XIII
CUCKOOS

1. HODGSON'S HAWK-CUCKOO, *Cuculus fugax*. 11'' (28cm).

   LARGE HAWK-CUCKOO, *Cuculus sparverioides*. 12'' (30cm). Like other Hawk-Cuckoos, but cheeks same colour as rest of head; chest rufous; breast barred. Mainly montane.

   INDIAN CUCKOO, *Cuculus micropterus*. 11'' (28cm). Grey-brown upperparts; grey head, throat and upper breast; belly whitish with black bars.

   ORIENTAL CUCKOO, *Cuculus saturatus*. 10-12'' (25-30cm). Dark grey upperparts, paler on side of head and throat, browner on wings; belly white shading to reddish buff posteriorly, barred dark brown. Mainly montane.

2. COMMON KOEL, *Eudynamys scolopacea,* a) Male, b) Female. 16'' (40cm). Migrant.

3. MOUSTACHED HAWK-CUCKOO, *Cuculus vagans*. 10'' (25cm). From Hodgson's Hawk-Cuckoo by black moustache; white tip to tail; smaller size.

4. PLAINTIVE CUCKOO, *Cacomantis merulinus*. 8'' (20cm). Immature very like Banded Bay Cuckoo adult, but with broader bands.

   BRUSH CUCKOO, *Cacomantis variolosus*. 9'' (23cm). Like Plaintive Cuckoo, but darker, eyering bright yellow.

5. BANDED BAY CUCKOO, *Cacomantis sonneratil*. 8'' (20cm).

6. VIOLET CUCKOO, *Chrysococcyx xanthorhynchus*. 6'' (15cm). Female like Malayan Bronze Cuckoo, but bill has red base, forehead and crown dark brown.

7. MALAYAN BRONZE CUCKOO, *Chrysococcyx minutillus* (formerly *malayanus*). 6'' (15cm). Dark green cap contrasting with white forecrown and paler back. Narrow bill.

   RUFOUS BRONZE CUCKOO, *Chrysococcyx russatus*. 6'' (15cm). Like Malayan Bronze Cuckoo, but cap same colour as back, forecrown dull grey. Broad bill.

   HORSFIELD'S BRONZE CUCKOO, *Chrysococcyx basalis*. 5¾'' (14cm). Like Malayan Bronze Cuckoo, but no white in forecrown, prominent whitish eyebrow, dark ear coverts. Vagrant.

8. DRONGO CUCKOO, *Surniculus lugubris*. 9'' (23cm). From drongos by thin bill, white bars in tail.

9. CHESTNUT-WINGED CUCKOO, *Clamator coromandus*. 15'' (38cm). Migrant.

PLATE XIII

PLATE XIV
MALKOHAS, COUCALS, AND GROUND-CUCKOO

1. RAFFLES'S MALKOHA, *Phaenicophaeus chlorophaeus.* a) Male, b) Female. 12'' (30cm).

2. BLACK-BELLIED MALKOHA, *Phaenicophaeus diardi.* 13'' (33cm).

3. CHESTNUT-BELLIED MALKOHA, *Phaenicophaeus sumatranus.* 13'' (33cm).

4. RED-BILLED MALKOHA, *Phaenicophaeus javanicus.* 17'' (43cm).

5. CHESTNUT-BREASTED MALKOHA, *Phaenicophaeus curvirostris.* 17'' (43cm).

6. LESSER COUCAL, *Centropus bengalensis.* 14'' (35cm). Wing lining chestnut. Immature all reddish brown with buffy streaks. Secondary scrub.

7. SHORT-TOED COUCAL, *Centropus rectunguis.* 13'' (33cm). Wing lining black. Primary forest.

8. COMMON (GREATER) COUCAL, *Centropus sinensis.* 21'' (53cm). Secondary scrub.

9. GROUND-CUCKOO, *Carpococcyx radiceus.* 24'' (61cm).

PLATE XIV

1a

1b

2

3

4

5

6

7

8

9

0"   3"   6"
0   50   mm 100   150

Ann Hughes
1956

PLATE XV
OWLS

1. BAY OWL, *Phodilus badius.* 10'' (25cm).

2. REDDISH SCOPS-OWL, *Otus rufescens.* 7'' (18cm).

3. MOUNTAIN SCOPS-OWL, *Otus spilocephalus.* 7'' (18cm). Montane.

4. COMMON (MANTANANI) SCOPS-OWL, *Otus scops mantananensis.* 7'' (18cm). Mantanani Island only.

5. COLLARED SCOPS-OWL, *Otus bakkamoena.* 8'' (20cm).

6. RAJAH'S SCOPS-OWL, *Otus brookei.* 9'' (23cm). Montane. Rare.

7. BROWN HAWK-OWL, *Ninox scutulata.* 10'' (25cm).

8. BARRED EAGLE-OWL, *Bubo sumatrana.* 18'' (46cm).

9. BROWN WOOD OWL, *Strix leptogrammica.* 16'' (41cm).

10. BUFFY FISH-OWL, *Ketupa ketupu.* 18'' (46cm).

11. COLLARED OWLET, *Glaucidium brodiei.* 6'' (15cm). Montane.

    SHORT-EARED OWL, *Asio flammeus.* 15'' (38cm). Tawny brown with dark bars. Diurnal flier in open grassy areas. Vagrant.

PLATE XV

1

2

3

4

5

6

7

8

9

10

11

Aw Hughes
1956

PLATE XVI
FROGMOUTHS AND NIGHTJARS

1. LARGE FROGMOUTH, *Batrachostomus auritus*. 17'' (43cm). Wing > 260mm.

2.* DULIT FROGMOUTH, *Batrachostomus harterti*. 13'' (34cm). Wing 220-250mm. Montane.

3. GOULD'S FROGMOUTH, *Batrachostomus stellatus*. 8½'' (22cm). Wing 115-130mm, tail slightly shorter than wing.

4. SUNDA FROGMOUTH, *Batrachostomus cornutus*. 9½'' (24cm). Colour variable. Wing 130-145mm. Tail slightly longer than wing.

5. BLYTH'S (JAVAN) FROGMOUTH, *Batrachostomus javensis*. 7½'' (19cm). Wing about 120mm, tail shorter than wing.

6. PALE-HEADED FROGMOUTH, *Batrachostomus poliolophus*. 8'' (20cm). Wing 115-130mm. No pale cross-bars in tail. Montane.

7. MALAYSIAN EARED NIGHTJAR, *Eurostopodus temminckii*. 11'' (28cm). No white in wing or tail; whistled call 'tok tadau' during flight.

8. SAVANNA NIGHTJAR, *Caprimulgus affinis*. 8'' (20cm). White in wing. Male: outer 2 tail feathers all white. Female: tail all dark.

9. BONAPARTE'S NIGHTJAR, *Caprimulgus concretus*. 8'' (20cm). No white in wings.

10. LARGE-TAILED NIGHTJAR, *Caprimulgus macrurus*. 11'' (28cm). Male: prominent white patch in wing and tail. Female: white replaced by buff. Call a deep 'chonk' repeated frequently.

   GREY NIGHTJAR, *Caprimulgus indicus*. 11'' (28cm). Similar to Large-tailed Nightjar but greyer. Male: white on outer four tail feathers forms a distinct subterminal band. Female: white replaced by buff. Migrant.

PLATE **XVI**

AmHughes
1956

PLATE XVII
SWIFTS AND SWALLOWS

1. BLACK-NEST SWIFTLET, *Collocalia maxima.* 4½'' (11cm). Wing 129-137mm; uniform dark brown above.

   GIANT SWIFTLET, *Collocalia gigas.* 5½'' (14cm). Wing 157-162mm; like Black-nest Swiftlet, but larger. Migrant.

   MOSSY-NEST SWIFTLET, *Collocalia vanikorensis.* 4'' (10cm). Wing 116-125mm; like Black-nest Swiftlet, but smaller, tarsus unfeathered.

   BROWN-RUMPED (EDIBLE-NEST) SWIFTLET, *Collocalia vestita.* 4'' (10cm). Very like Mossy-nest Swiftlet, but bases of rump feathers are white not brown. Usually considered conspecific with next species.

   GREY-RUMPED (EDIBLE-NEST) SWIFTLET, *Collocalia fuciphaga.* 4'' (10cm). Like Brown-rumped Swiftlet, but rump is paler than back.

2. BROWN SPINETAILED SWIFT (NEEDLETAIL), *Hirundapus giganteus.* 8½'' (22cm).

   WHITE-THROATED SPINETAILED SWIFT (NEEDLETAIL), *Hirundapus caudacutus.* 7'' (18cm). Like Brown Needletail, but forehead, throat and tertials white. Lower back pale. Migrant.

3. WHITE-BELLIED SWIFTLET, *Collocalia esculenta.* 3½'' (9cm).

4. HOUSE SWIFT, *Apus affinis.* 5'' (13cm).

   FORK-TAILED SWIFT, *Apus pacificus.* 6'' (15cm). Like House Swift, but slightly larger with deeply forked tail. Migrant.

5. ASIAN PALM SWIFT, *Cypsiurus balasiensis.* 4½'' (11cm). From swiftlets by longer, forked tail.

6. SILVER-RUMPED SWIFT, *Raphidura leucopygialis.* 4'' (10cm).

7. CRESTED (GREY-RUMPED) TREESWIFT, *Hemiprocne longipennis.* 8'' (20cm).

8. WHISKERED TREESWIFT, *Hemiprocne comata.* 6'' (15cm).

9. PACIFIC SWALLOW, *Hirundo tahitica.* 5'' (13cm).

   COMMON (BARN) SWALLOW, *Hirundo rustica.* 5½'' (14cm). Like Pacific Swallow, but black collar below rufous throat. Migrant.

   RED-RUMPED SWALLOW, *Hirundo daurica.* 7'' (18cm). Like Pacific Swallow, but longer black tail, rufous rump, lightly streaked underparts, slower flight. Migrant.

   SAND MARTIN, *Riparia riparia.* 4½'' (12cm). Brown upperparts, white underparts with brown chest band. Migrant.

   ASIAN HOUSE MARTIN, *Delichon dasypus.* 5'' (13cm). Blackish upperparts with pure white rump and underparts. Migrant.

PLATE XVII

Am Hughes
1957

PLATE XVIII
TROGONS

1. DIARD'S TROGON, *Harpactes diardii.* a) Male, b) Female. 12''
    (30cm). Mauve facial skin.

2. SCARLET-RUMPED TROGON, *Harpactes duvaucelii.* a) Male,
    b) Female. 9'' (23cm).

3. RED-NAPED TROGON, *Harpactes kasumba.* a) Male,
    b) Female. 12'' (30cm). Blue facial skin.

4.* WHITEHEAD'S TROGON, *Harpactes whiteheadi.* a) Male,
    b) Female. 12'' (30cm). Montane.

5. ORANGE-BREASTED TROGON, *Harpactes oreskios.* a) Male, b)
    Female. 10'' (25cm). Montane.

6. CINNAMON-RUMPED TROGON, *Harpactes orrhophaeus.*
    a) Male, b) Female. 10'' (25cm). Female from Scarlet-rumped
    Trogon female by absence of pink in plumage; contrasting rusty
    feathers around eye.

PLATE XVIII

1a   1b   2a   2b   3a   3b

4a   4b   5a   5b   6a   6b

AmHughes
1956

PLATE XIX
KINGFISHERS

1. BANDED KINGFISHER, *Lacedo pulchella,* a) Male, b) Female. 8''
   (20cm).

2. CHESTNUT (RUFOUS) - COLLARED KINGFISHER, *Halcyon concreta.* 9'' (23cm). Female has green back with buff spots.

3. WHITE-COLLARED (COLLARED) KINGFISHER, *Halcyon chloris.* 9'' (23cm).

   SACRED KINGFISHER, *Halcyon sancta.* 8'' (20cm). Like White-collared but smaller with buffy forehead and buffy wash on underparts. Rare migrant.

4. RUDDY KINGFISHER, *Halcyon coromanda.* 9'' (23cm).

5. BLACK-CAPPED KINGFISHER, *Halcyon pileata.* 10'' (25cm). Migrant.

6. STORK-BILLED KINGFISHER, *Pelargopsis capensis.* 13''
   (33cm).

7. BLUE-EARED KINGFISHER, *Alcedo meninting.* 6'' (15cm).

8. BLUE-BANDED KINGFISHER, *Alcedo euryzona.* 7'' (18cm). Female like Blue-eared Kingfisher but larger, duller, with blackish wings.

9. COMMON KINGFISHER, *Alcedo atthis.* 6'' (15cm). Migrant.

10. BLACK-BACKED KINGFISHER, *Ceyx erithacus.* 6'' (15cm).

11. RUFOUS-BACKED KINGFISHER, *Ceyx rufidorsus.* 6'' (15cm). Usually considered conspecific with Black-backed Kingfisher as intergrades occur.

PLATE XIX

Aun Hughes
1956

PLATE XX
HORNBILLS

1. WHITE-CRESTED (WHITE-CROWNED) HORNBILL, *Berenicornis comatus*. a) Male, b) Female. 34'' (85cm).

2. WREATHED HORNBILL, *Rhyticeros undulatus*. 36'' (90cm).

3. WRINKLED HORNBILL, *Rhyticeros corrugatus*. 27'' (70cm). Tail often white; from Wreathed by smaller size; raised casque; dark base to tail.

4. BUSHY-CRESTED HORNBILL, *Anorrhinus galeritus*. 27'' (70cm).

5. BLACK HORNBILL, *Anthracoceros malayanus*. 29'' (75cm).

6. HELMETED HORNBILL, *Rhinoplax vigil*. 50'' (125cm).

7. RHINOCEROS HORNBILL, *Buceros rhinoceros*. 42'' (105cm).

8. PIED HORNBILL, *Anthrococeros coronatus*. 30'' (75cm).

PLATE XX

PLATE XXI
BARBETS

(The barbets, except the first species, have plain green bodies and live in the forest canopy. The most distinctive calls of each are described to aid in identification.)

1. BROWN BARBET, *Calorhamphus fuliginosus*. 7'' (18cm). Grey-brown back, buffy underparts.

2. YELLOW-CROWNED BARBET, *Megalaima henricii*. 8'' (20cm). Call 'trrrook--took-took-took-took'.

3.* BLACK-THROATED BARBET, *Megalaima eximia*. Immature Male. 6'' (15cm). Adult Male has a black chin and upper throat; red patch on lower throat. Call a very rapid unbroken series of 'took' notes. Montane.

4. GAUDY (RED-THROATED) BARBET, *Megalaima mystacophanos*. a) Male, b) Female. 8'' (20cm). Call a series of 1 or 2 note 'toc's with irregular gaps.

5. LITTLE (BLUE-EARED) BARBET, *Megalaima australis*. 6'' (15cm). Call 'to-rook to-rook' repeated continuously.

6. MANY-COLOURED (RED-CROWNED) BARBET, *Megalaima rafflesii*. 10'' (25cm). Call 'took-took (pause) took-took-took.. (10-15 notes)'.

7. GOLD-WHISKERED BARBET, *Megalaima chrysopogon*. 10'' (25cm). Call 'tu-whoop' repeated 30-50 times.

8.* GOLDEN-NAPED BARBET, *Megalaima pulcherrima*. 8'' (20cm). Call 'took-took-trrrook' repeated often. Montane.

9.* MOUNTAIN BARBET, *Megalaima monticola*. 9'' (23cm). Call a rapid series of 'took' notes with irregular hiccups. Montane.

PLATE XXI

1

2

3

4a

4b

5

6

7

8

9

AₘHughes
— 1956

PLATE XXII
WOODPECKERS

1. CHECKER-THROATED WOODPECKER, *Picus mentalis.* 11''
(28cm).

2. CRIMSON-WINGED WOODPECKER, *Picus puniceus.* 9'' (23cm).

3. BANDED WOODPECKER, *Picus miniaceus.* 10'' (25cm).

4. GOLDEN-BACKED THREE-TOED WOODPECKER (COMMON
GOLDENBACK), *Dinopium javanense.* 9'' (23cm).

5. CRIMSON-BACKED FOUR-TOED WOODPECKER (GREATER
GOLDENBACK), *Chrysocolaptes lucidus.* 11'' (28cm). From
Common Goldenback by larger size, heavier bill and double malar
stripe. E. Sabah only.

6. GREAT SLATY WOODPECKER, *Mulleripicus pulverulentus.* 17''
(43cm).

7. GREAT BLACK (WHITE-BELLIED) WOODPECKER, *Dryocopus
javensis.* 17'' (43cm).

8. OLIVE-BACKED WOODPECKER, *Dinopium rafflesi.* 10'' (25cm).

9. ORANGE-BACKED WOODPECKER, *Chrysocolaptes validus.*
a) Male, b) Female. 11'' (28cm).

PLATE XXII

1

2

3

4

5

6

7

8

9a

9b

0"   3"   6"

0   50   mm 100   150

A. Hughes
1956

PLATE XXIII
WOODPECKERS

1. RUFOUS WOODPECKER, *Micropternus brachyurus.* 9'' (23cm).

2. MAROON WOODPECKER, *Blythipicus rubiginosus.* 8'' (20cm).

3. RUFOUS PICULET, *Sasia abnormis.* 3½'' (9cm).

4. SPECKLED PICULET, *Picumnus innominatus.* 4'' (10cm).

5. GREY-AND-BUFF WOODPECKER, *Hemicircus concretus.* 5'' (13cm).

6. BUFF-RUMPED WOODPECKER, *Meiglyptes tristis.* 6'' (15cm). Has a distinct crest.

7. GREY-CAPPED WOODPECKER, *Picoides canicapillus.* 3½'' (14cm).

8. BUFF-NECKED WOODPECKER, *Meiglyptes tukki.* 8'' (20cm).

9. BROWN-CAPPED WOODPECKER, *Picoides moluccensis.* 5½'' (14cm). From Grey-capped Woodpecker by browner crown and upperparts, unmarked throat, broad dark malar stripe.

PLATE XXIII

A Hughes
1956

PLATE XXIV
BROADBILLS

1.* HOSE'S BROADBILL, *Calyptomena hosei*. 8'' (20cm). Submontane.

2. GREEN BROADBILL, *Calyptomena viridis*. 6'' (15cm).

3.* WHITEHEAD'S BROADBILL, *Calyptomena whiteheadi*. 10'' (25cm). Montane.

4. LONG-TAILED BROADBILL, *Psarisomus dalhousiae*. 10'' (25cm). Montane.

5. BLACK-AND-YELLOW BROADBILL, *Eurylaimus ochromalus*. 6'' (15cm).

6. BLACK-AND-RED BROADBILL, *Cymbirhynchus macrorhynchus*. 8'' (20cm).

7. BANDED BROADBILL, *Eurylaimus javanicus*. 8'' (20cm).

8. DUSKY BROADBILL, *Corydon sumatranus*. 9'' (23cm).

PLATE XXIV

Aw Hughes
1957

PLATE XXV
PITTAS

1.* BLUE-BANDED PITTA, *Pitta arquata*. 6'' (15cm). Submontane.

2. GIANT PITTA, *Pitta caerulea*. a) Male, b) Female. 11'' (28 cm).

3.* BLUE-HEADED PITTA, *Pitta baudi*. a) Male, b) Female. 7'' (18cm).

4. GARNET PITTA, *Pitta granatina*. 6'' (15cm).

5. HOODED PITTA, *Pitta sordida*. 6'' (15cm).

6. BANDED PITTA, *Pitta guajana*. 8'' (20cm).

7. BLUE-WINGED PITTA, *Pitta moluccensis*. 7'' (18cm). Migrant.

FAIRY PITTA, *Pitta nympha*. 7'' (18cm). Like Blue-winged Pitta, but long narrow buffy white eyebrow; smaller white wing patch; darker underparts. Migrant.

MANGROVE PITTA, *Pitta megarhyncha*. 7'' (18cm). Very like Blue-winged Pitta, but dark crown stripe absent, larger bill. Rare.

PLATE XXV

PLATE XXVI
GREYBIRDS, TRILLER AND SHRIKES

1. BAR-BELLIED CUCKOO-SHRIKE, *Coracina striata.* 10'' (25cm). Female barred on whole rear half of body.

2. BAR-WINGED FLYCATCHER-SHRIKE, *Hemipus picatus.* 5'' (13cm).

3. BLACK-FACED CUCKOO-SHRIKE, *Coracina larvata.* 9'' (23cm). Montane.

4. LARGE WOOD-SHRIKE, *Tephrodornis virgatus.* 7'' (18cm). Female browner.

5. BLACK-WINGED FLYCATCHER-SHRIKE, *Hemipus hirundinaceus.* 5'' (13cm).

6. LESSER CUCKOO-SHRIKE, *Coracina fimbriata.* 7'' (18cm). Female paler with finely barred underparts.

7. BROWN SHRIKE, *Lanius cristatus.* 7'' (18cm). Migrant.

8. PIED TRILLER, *Lalage nigra.* 6½'' (17cm). Female browner with light barring below.

9. LONG-TAILED SHRIKE, *Lanius schach.* 9'' (23cm). Dark wings with white patch and long tail. In some races top of crown and nape grey. Rare migrant.

10. THICK-BILLED (TIGER) SHRIKE, *Lanius tigrinus.* 6½'' (17cm). Immature like Brown Shrike, but indistinct black mask. Migrant.

PLATE XXVI

Aun Hughes
1957

0"   3"   6"
0   50   mm   100   150

PLATE XXVIA
WAGTAILS, PIPITS and Larks

1. FOREST WAGTAIL, *Dendronanthus indicus.* 6'' (15cm). From White Wagtail by brown upperparts. Migrant.

2. GREY WAGTAIL, *Motacilla cinerea.* 8'' (20cm). From Yellow Wagtail by longer tail; grey upperparts; bright yellow undertail coverts. Migrant.

3. RED-THROATED PIPIT, *Anthus cervinus.* a) summer plumage, b) winter plumage. 5½'' (14cm). Call a thin 'seep'. Migrant.

4. YELLOW WAGTAIL, *Motacilla flava simillima.* a) Adult, b) Immature. 7'' (18cm). This race has a grey crown. Migrant.

5. WHITE WAGTAIL, *Motacilla alba.* 8'' (20cm). Variable amounts of black and grey in plumage. Migrant.

6. YELLOW WAGTAIL, *Motacilla flava taivana.* 7'' (18cm). This race has an olive crown. Migrant.

7. RICHARD'S PIPIT, *Anthus novaeseelandiae.* 6'' (15cm). Lightly streaked underparts.

   OLIVE TREE PIPIT, *Anthus hodgsoni.* 6'' (15cm). Olive upperparts; white underparts with heavy black streaking. Migrant.

   PETCHORA PIPIT, *Anthus gustavi.* 5½'' (14cm). Like Red-throated Pipit in winter, but white·'V' on back; call a hard 'pwit'. Migrant.

   SKYLARK, *Alauda arvensis.* 6½'' (16cm). Upperparts brown with black streaks; underparts white with dark streaks; white outer tail feathers; slight crest; thicker bill than pipits. Migrant.

   (SINGING) BUSH LARK, *Mirafra javanica.* 5'' (13cm). Reddish brown above, mottled with black; pale below, streaked with black; short tail. S. Borneo only.

4a   4b   5   6   7

PLATE XXVII
MINIVETS AND WOOD-SWALLOW

1. ASHY MINIVET, *Pericrocotus divaricatus.* a) Male, b) Female. 7'' (18cm). Migrant.

2. MOUNTAIN (GREY-CHINNED) MINIVET, *Pericrocotus solaris.* a) Male, b) Female. 6½'' (16cm). Male from other minivets by dark grey not black throat. Montane.

3. FIERY MINIVET, *Pericrocotus igneus.* a) Male, b) Female. 5½'' (14cm)

4. SCARLET MINIVET, *Pericrocotus flammeus.* a) Male, b) Female. 6'' (15cm). Male from Fiery Minivet by red spot on secondaries, larger size.

5. WHITE-BREASTED WOOD-SWALLOW, *Artamus leucorhynchus.* 7'' (18cm).

PLATE XXVII

1b   1a

2b

2a

3a   3b

4b

4a

5

0"   1"   2"   3"

0   25 mm 50   75

PLATE XXVIII
IORAS, LEAFBIRDS AND BLUEBIRD

1. GREEN IORA, *Aegithina viridissima*. 5'' (13cm). Forest.

2. COMMON IORA, *Aegithina tiphia*. 5'' (13cm). Mangrove and gardens.

3. GREATER GREEN LEAFBIRD, *Chloropsis sonnerati*. a) Male, b) Female. 7½'' (19cm). From Lesser Green Leafbird by larger bill, yellow throat in female.

4. LESSER GREEN LEAFBIRD, *Chloropsis cyanopogon*. a) Male, b) Female. 6½'' (16cm).

5. BLUE-WINGED LEAFBIRD, *Chloropsis cochinchinensis*. a) Male, b) Female. 7'' (18cm). Montane race female has a black throat.

6. (ASIAN) FAIRY BLUEBIRD, *Irena puella*. a) Male, b) Female. 9'' (23cm).

PLATE XXVIII

Am Hughes
1957

PLATE XXIX
BULBULS

1. BLACK-HEADED BULBUL, *Pycnonotus atriceps*. 6'' (15cm).

2. BLACK-CRESTED BULBUL, *Pycnonotus melanicterus*. 7'' (17cm). Montane.

3. SCALY-BREASTED BULBUL, *Pycnonotus squamatus*. 6'' (15cm).

4. GREY-BELLIED BULBUL, *Pycnonotus cyaniventris*. 6'' (15cm).

5. STRAW-HEADED BULBUL, *Pycnonotus zeylanicus*. 10'' (25cm).

6. PALE-FACED (FLAVESCENT) BULBUL, *Pycnonotus flavescens*. 7'' (17cm). Montane.

7. YELLOW-VENTED BULBUL, *Pycnonotus goiavier*. 7'' (17cm). Dark line through eye, paler vent than Pale-faced Bulbul. Lowland gardens and scrub.

8. GREY-CHEEKED BULBUL, *Criniger bres*. 8'' (20cm).

9. YELLOW-BELLIED BULBUL, *Criniger phaeocephalus*. 7½'' (18cm). Sabah race has no yellow band on tail.

10. FINSCH'S BULBUL, *Criniger finschii*. 6½'' (16cm).

11. OCHRACEOUS BULBUL, *Criniger ochraceus*. 8'' (20cm). From Grey-cheeked Bulbul by darker underparts; browner undertail coverts. Montane.

PLATE XXIX

1

2

3

4

5

6

7

8

9

10

11

AHughes
1957

PLATE XXX
BULBULS

1. PUFF-BACKED BULBUL, *Pycnonotus eutilotus*. 8'' (20cm).

2. NIEUWENHUIS'S BULBUL, *Pycnonotus nieuwenhuisi*. 7'' (18cm). Rare.

3. BLACK-AND-WHITE BULBUL, *Pycnonotus melanoleucos*. 6½'' (17cm).

4. OLIVE-WINGED BULBUL, *Pycnonotus plumosus*. 7'' (18cm). Larger than other brown bulbuls with contrasting greenish wings and tail; streaked ear coverts.

5. RED-EYED BULBUL, *Pycnonotus brunneus*. 7'' (18cm). Eye orange-red.

   CREAM-VENTED BULBUL, *Pycnonotus simplex*. 7'' (18cm). Very like Red-eyed, but vent and throat creamier white; eye white or dark red.

6. SPECTACLED BULBUL, *Pycnonotus erythropthalmos*. 6½'' (17cm). From Red-eyed by smaller size and narrow yellow-orange eyering.

7. HOOK-BILLED BULBUL, *Setornis criniger*. 7½'' (19cm).

8. HAIRY-BACKED BULBUL, *Hypsipetes criniger*. 6'' (15cm). Yellowish face.

9. STREAKED BULBUL, *Hypsipetes malaccensis*. 8'' (20cm).

10. BUFF-VENTED BULBUL, *Hypsipetes charlottae*. 7'' (18cm). Pale grey eye; slight buffy eyebrow.

11. ASHY BULBUL, *Hypsipetes flavala*. 8'' (20cm). White throat. From Ochraceus Bulbul by greyer plumage, yellow on wings and under tail. Montane.

PLATE XXX

Hughes 1957

PLATE XXXI
THRUSHES, FORKTAILS, LAUGHINGTHRUSHES
and Chats

1. RUFOUS-TAILED SHAMA, *Copyschus pyrrhopyga*. 8" (20cm).

 2. WHITE-RUMPED SHAMA, *Copysychus malabaricus*. 11" (28cm). Sabah race has a white crown.

3. MAGPIE-ROBIN, *Copyschus saularis*. 8" (20cm). Northern race has black belly; Southeastern race is all black.

4. WHITE-CROWNED FORKTAIL, *Enicurus leschenaulti*. 8" (20cm).

5. CHESTNUT-NAPED FORKTAIL, *Enicurus ruficapillus*. 7" (18cm).

6. BLUE ROCK THRUSH, *Monticola solitarius*. 8" (20cm). a) Male, b) Female. Migrant.

WHITE'S (SCALY) THRUSH, *Zoothera dauma*. 11" (28cm). Olive brown upperparts; buffy breast and white belly covered all over with crescentic black scales; white wing bar. Vagrant.

7. EYE-BROWED THRUSH, *Turdus obscurus*. 10" (25cm). Usually has white eyebrow. Female has a whitish throat with brown streaks. Migrant.

8. SUNDA WHISTLING THRUSH, *Myophonus glaucinus*. 9" (23cm).

9. BLACK LAUGHINGTHRUSH, *Garrulax lugubris*. 10" (25cm). Montane.

10. CHESTNUT-CAPPED LAUGHINGTHRUSH, *Garrulax mitratus*. 10" (25cm). Montane.

11. GREY-AND-BROWN LAUGHINGTHRUSH, *Garrulax palliatus*. 10" (25cm). Montane.

SIBERIAN BLUE ROBIN, *Erithacus cyane*. 5" (13cm). Male dark blue above; pure white below. Female brown above; whitish below; mottled breast. Long pink legs; wags tail. Migrant.

ORANGE-FLANKED BUSH ROBIN, *Tarsiger cyanurus*. 6" (15cm). Male dark blue above with shiny blue forehead; white below with orange flank patch. Female: blue replaced by brown except on tail. Vagrant.

WHEATEAR, *Oenanthe oenanthe*. 5¾" (14cm). Sandy buff with dark wings and tail; white rump and base of tail. Open fields. Vagrant.

STONECHAT, *Saxicola torquata*. 5" (13cm). Male: black head; brownish body; white patches on shoulder, wing and rump. Female: buffy brown below; streaked brown above; white wing patch. Perches upright and flicks tail. Rare migrant.

PIED (BUSH) CHAT, *Saxicola caprata*. 5½" (14cm). Male black with white patches in wings and tail coverts. Female dark brown all over except rusty rump. Vagrant.

PLATE XXXI

PLATE XXXII
SOME BIRDS OF MT. KINABALU

1.* SHORT-TAILED BUSH WARBLER, *Cettia whiteheadi*. 3¾"
(9cm). Montane.

✓ 2.* MOUNTAIN BLACKEYE, *Chlorocharis emiliae*. 4½" (11cm).
Montane.

3. MOUNTAIN BUSH WARBLER, *Cettia vulcania*. 5" (13cm).
Montane.

4. MOUNTAIN LEAF WARBLER, *Phylloscopus trivirgatus*. 4"
(10cm). Some birds are much yellower. Montane.

5.* BORNEAN MOUNTAIN WHISTLER, *Pachycephala hypoxantha*.
6½" (16cm). Montane.

6. YELLOW-BREASTED WARBLER, *Seicercus montis*. 4" (10cm).
Montane.

7. BLUE (WHITE-BROWED) SHORTWING, *Brachypteryx
montana*. 5½" (14cm). Montane.

8.* KINABALU FRIENDLY WARBLER, *Bradypterus accentor*. 6"
(15cm). Montane.

9.* PYGMY WHITE-EYE, *Oculocincta squamifrons*. 6" (15cm).
Submontane.

10. MOUNTAIN BLACKBIRD, *Turdus poliocephalus*. 9" (23cm).
Montane.

11.* BLACK-BREASTED TRILLER, *Chlamydochaera jefferyi*. 9"
(23cm). Montane.

PLATE XXXII

PLATE XXXIII
BABBLERS

1. (MALAYSIAN) RAIL-BABBLER, *Eupetes macrocerus.* 10'' (25cm).

2. BLACK-CAPPED BABBLER, *Pellorneum capistratum.* 6'' (15cm).

3. TEMMINCK'S BABBLER, *Trichastoma pyrrhogenys.* 5½'' (14cm). Streaking on crown; mottled cheeks; variable rufous on chest. Submontane.

4. SHORT-TAILED BABBLER, *Trichastoma malaccense.* 5'' (13cm). Black moustachial stripe.

5. WHITE-CHESTED BABBLER, *Trichastoma rostratum.* 5½'' (14cm). Plain brown above, all white below.

6. FERRUGINOUS BABBLER, *Trichastoma bicolor.* 6½'' (17cm). Uniform reddish brown above.

7. HORSFIELD'S BABBLER, *Trichastoma sepiarium.* 5½'' (14cm).

8. ABBOTT'S BABBLER, *Trichastoma abbotti.* 5½'' (14cm). Secondary scrub.

9. BROWN FULVETTA, *Alcippe brunneicauda.* 5½'' (14cm).

10. WHITE-BELLIED YUHINA, *Yuhina zantholeuca.* 4½'' (11cm).

PLATE XXXIII

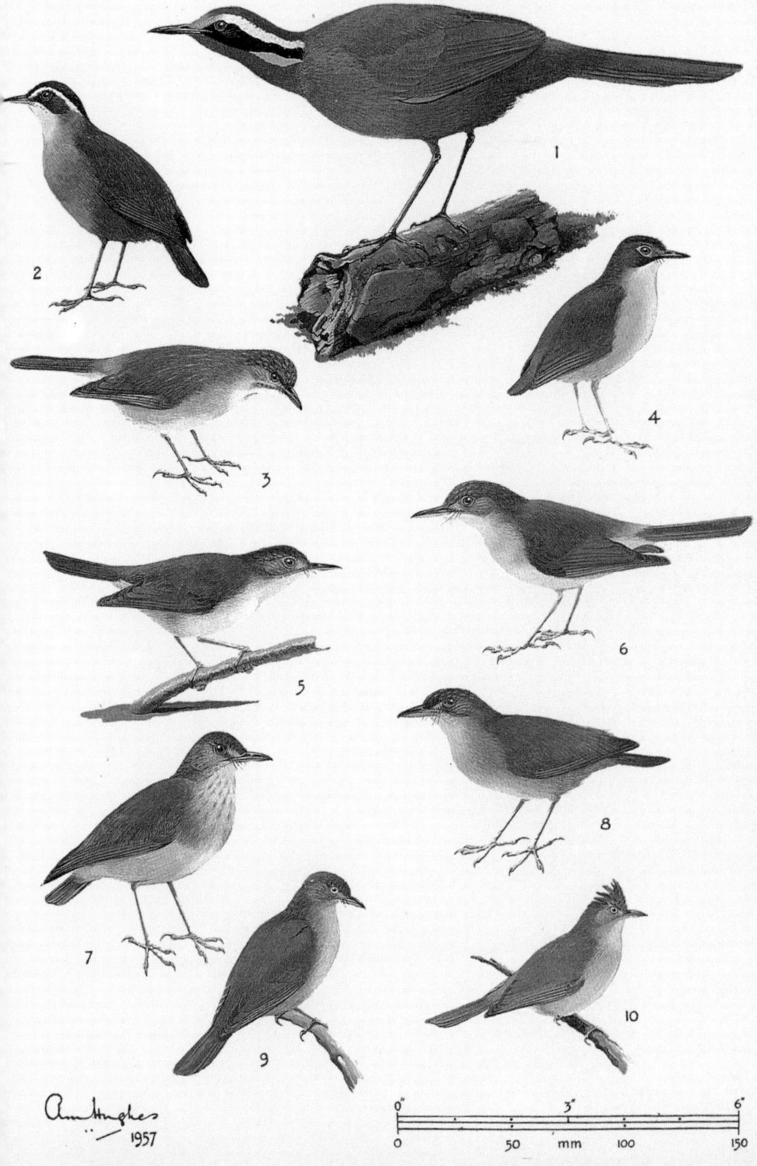

Aw Hughes
1957

0"   3"   6"
0   50   mm   100   150

PLATE XXXIV
BABBLERS

1. RUFOUS-CROWNED BABBLER, *Malacopteron magnum.* 6½"
(17cm).

2. SCALY-CROWNED BABBLER, *Malacopteron cinereum.* 6"
(15cm). From Rufous-crowned by smaller size, unstreaked breast
and black scales on forehead.

3. MOUSTACHED BABBLER, *Malacopteron magnirostre.* 6"
(15cm). Moustache sometimes indistinct.

4. PLAIN (SOOTY-CAPPED) BABBLER, *Malacopteron affine.* 6"
(15cm). From Moustached by darker cap, pale eyebrow.

5. CHESTNUT-BACKED SCIMITAR BABBLER, *Pomatorhinus
montanus.* 7½" (19cm).

6. WHITE-THROATED (GREY-BREASTED) BABBLER,
Malacopteron albogulare. 5" (13cm).

7.* BORNEAN WREN-BABBLER, *Ptilocichla leucogrammica.* 6"
(15cm).

8.* BLACK-THROATED WREN-BABBLER, *Napothera atrigularis.*
7" (18cm).

9. STRIPED WREN-BABBLER, *Kenopia striata.* 5½" (14cm).

10.* MOUNTAIN WREN-BABBLER, *Napothera crassa.* 5½" (14cm).
Montane.

11. SMALL (EYE-BROWED) WREN-BABBLER, *Napothera
epilepidota.* 4½" (12cm). Montane.

PLATE XXXIV

1

2

3

4

5

6

7

8

9

10

11

Alan Hughes
1957

0"   3   6

0   50   mm   100   150

PLATE XXXV
BABBLERS

1. FLUFFY-BACKED TIT-BABBLER, *Macronous ptilosus.* 6''
   (15cm).

2. STRIPED TIT-BABBLER, *Macronous gularis.* 6'' (15cm).

3. GREY-THROATED BABBLER, *Stachyris nigriceps.* 5'' (13cm).
   Montane.

4. GREY-HEADED BABBLER, *Stachyris poliocephala.* 6'' (15cm).

5. BLACK-THROATED BABBLER, *Stachyris nigricollis.* 6'' (15cm).

6. WHITE-NECKED BABBLER, *Stachyris leucotis.* 6'' (15cm).

7. CHESTNUT-RUMPED BABBLER, *Stachyris maculata.* 6½''
   (16cm).

8. CHESTNUT-WINGED BABBLER, *Stachyris erythroptera.* 5''
   (13cm).

9. RUFOUS-FRONTED BABBLER, *Stachyris rufifrons.* 4½''
   (12cm).

10. CHESTNUT-CRESTED BABBLER, *Yuhina everetti.* 5½'' (14cm).
    Montane.

11. WHITE-BROWED SHRIKE-BABBLER, *Pteruthius flaviscapis.*
    6'' (15cm). Montane.

PLATE XXXV

THREE INCHES

0   25   50   75
75mm

PLATE XXXVI
WARBLERS

1. FLYEATER, *Gerygone sulphurea.* 3½'' (9cm). Usually in canopy of rainforest.

2. YELLOW-BELLIED WREN-WARBLER (PRINIA), *Prinia flaviventris.* 5'' (13cm). Unstreaked with longish tail. Reeds and grasses.

3. PALLAS'S GRASSHOPPER WARBLER, *Locustella certhiola.* 6'' (15cm). Wing 60-68mm. Migrant.

    MIDDENDORFF'S WARBLER, *Locustella ochotensis.* 6'' (15cm). Very similar to Pallas's, but upperparts almost unstreaked. Migrant.

    LANCEOLATED WARBLER, *Locustella lanceolata.* 5'' (13cm). Like Pallas's, but no white tips to tail. Wing 53-59mm. Migrant.

4. EASTERN GREAT REED WARBLER, *Acrocephalus orientalis.* 7'' (17cm). Migrant.

    CLAMOROUS REED WARBLER, *Acrocephalus stentoreus.* 7'' (17cm). Like Great Reed Warbler, but (in hand) 2nd primary shorter than 5th, not equal or longer. Migrant.

    STRIATED WARBLER, *Megalurus palustris.* 10'' (25cm). Heavily streaked black and brown above; buffy-grey below. Long, graduated tail.

5. YELLOW-BELLIED WARBLER, *Abroscopus superciliaris.* 4'' (10cm). Submontane.

6. ARCTIC WARBLER, *Phylloscopus borealis.* 4'' (10cm). Migrant.

7. RED-TAILED TAILORBIRD, *Orthotomus sericeus.* 5'' (12cm).

8. BLACK-NECKED (DARK-NECKED) TAILORBIRD, *Orthotomus atrogularis.* 4½'' (11cm). Immatures lack black on neck.

9. MOUNTAIN TAILORBIRD, *Orthotomus cuculatus.* 4'' (10cm). Montane.

10. RED-HEADED (ASHY) TAILORBIRD, *Orthotomus ruficeps.* 4½'' (11cm).

PLATE XXXVI

THREE INCHES

0 1 2 3

0 25 50 75

75mm

AmHughes
1957

PLATE XXXVII
FLYCATCHERS

1. SOOTY (DARK-SIDED) FLYCATCHER, *Muscicapa sibirica.* 5''
(13cm). Greyish brown; white eyering; streaked underparts; bill
small and black. Migrant.

   (ASIAN) BROWN FLYCATCHER, *Muscicapa latirostris.* 5''
(13cm). Like Sooty, but often browner; less streaked underneath;
yellow base to lower mandible. Mainly migratory.

   GREY-STREAKED FLYCATCHER, *Muscicapa griseisticta.* 6''
(15cm). Like Sooty, but white underparts heavily streaked with dark
grey or black. Migrant.

2. FERRUGINOUS FLYCATCHER, *Muscicapa ferruginea.* 5''
(13cm). Dark rufous rump and tail with buffy rufous flanks.
Migrant.

3. VERDITER FLYCATCHER, *Muscicapa thalassina.* 6'' (15cm).
Should be all greenish-blue. Female has dusky lores.

4. INDIGO FLYCATCHER, *Muscicapa indigo.* 6'' (15cm). White in
base of tail, lower belly whitish or buffy. Montane.

5. BLUE-AND-WHITE FLYCATCHER, *Cynoptila cyanomelana.*
6½'' (17cm). Male: white in base of tail, pure white belly. Female:
brown upperparts, pale brown underparts with buffy throat patch
and centre of belly. Migrant.

6. WHITE-TAILED FLYCATCHER, *Cyornis concreta.* 6½'' (17cm).
Male: grey abdomen; white undertail coverts; no white in tail in
Bornean race. Female brown with white patch on lower throat, some
white in tail. Submontane.

7. PALE BLUE FLYCATCHER, *Cyornis unicolor.* 6'' (15cm).
Should be all pale blue with a greyish belly; buffy wining lining.
Female: dark brown back; greyish brown underparts.

8. MALAYSIAN BLUE FLYCATCHER, *Cyornis turcosa.* 5½''
(14cm). Female very similar to Bornean Blue male, but duller
underparts; less shiny forehead.

9. MANGROVE BLUE FLYCATCHER, *Cyornis rufigastra.* 5½''
(14cm). Male: black point to chin; dull blue upperparts; whitish
belly. Female similar but lores white.

10. LARGE-BILLED BLUE FLYCATCHER, *Cyornis caerulata.* 5½''
(14cm). Male like Mangrove Blue Flycatcher, but shiny forehead,
brighter blue upperparts. Female brown above with blue rump and
tail.

Continued on next page

PLATE XXXVII

Am Hughes
1958

11. HILL BLUE FLYCATCHER, *Cyornis banyumas.* 5½'' (14cm). Male: light blue forehead; dull blue upperparts; uniform rufous underparts. Female all brown above.

12.* BORNEAN BLUE FLYCATCHER, *Cyornis superba.* 6'' (15cm). Male: pale chin, shiny blue forehead and rump. Female: reddish brown above, brightest on forehead, rump and tail.

13. SNOWY-BROWED FLYCATCHER, *Ficedula hyperythra.* 4'' (10cm). White base to dark tail. Female greyish brown above, buff throat and belly. Montane.

14. MUGIMAKI FLYCATCHER, *Ficedula mugimaki.* 5'' (12cm). Male: black or grey upperparts; white base to tail; large white patch in wings. Female dull brown above; whitish wing bars; buffy throat. Migrant.

15. RUFOUS-CHESTED FLYCATCHER, *Ficedula dumetoria.* 4½'' (11cm). Male: black upperparts except white eyebrow, wing bar and base to tail; chin paler than throat. Female olive brown above with whitish wing patch.

RED-BREASTED (THROATED) FLYCATCHER, *Ficedula parva* 5'' (12cm). Plain brown above, paler below; black tail with white base. Male: orange red throat. Rare migrant.

16. NARCISSUS FLYCATCHER, *Ficedula narcissina.* 5'' (13cm). Male: white patch in wing; bright yellow rump; whitish belly. Female: olive brown back and rump; rufous brown wings and tail; pale buff underparts. Migrant.

17. LITTLE PIED FLYCATCHER, *Ficedula westermanni.* 4'' (10cm). Male: white patch on wing and base to tail. Female: olive brown above; rufous brown rump; underparts whitish with greyer sides. Montane.

18. PYGMY BLUE FLYCATCHER, *Muscicapella hodgsoni.* 3½'' (9cm). Thin narrow bill. Female olive brown above; buffy white below. Montane.

19. GREY-HEADED FLYCATCHER, *Culicicapa ceylonensis.* 4½'' (11cm). Yellow belly; greenish back; grey head.

20. BLACK-NAPED MONARCH, *Hypothymis azurea.* 5'' (13cm). Long blue tail. Female greyer; lacks black crest and breast band.

NOTES

PLATE XXXVIII
FLYCATCHERS, WHISTLER AND NUTHATCH

1. WHITE-THROATED FANTAIL, *Rhipidura albicollis*. 7'' (18cm). Montane.

2. SPOTTED FANTAIL, *Rhipidura perlata*. 7'' (18cm).

3. PIED FANTAIL, *Rhipidura javanica*. 6½'' (17cm).

4. ASIAN PARADISE FLYCATCHER, *Terpsiphone paradisi*. a) Male, b) Female. 8'' (20cm). Male tail up to 10'' (25cm) longer.

5. WHITE-THROATED (GREY-CHESTED) JUNGLE FLYCATCHER, *Rhinomyias umbratilis*. 6'' (15cm). Breast band greyish.

6. RUFOUS-TAILED JUNGLE FLYCATCHER, *Rhinomyias ruficauda*. 5½'' (14cm). Indistinct breast band; rufous tail. Submontane.

   OLIVE-BACKED (FULVOUS-CHESTED) JUNGLE FLYCATCHER, *Rhinomyias olivacea*. 5½'' (14cm). Like Grey-chested but breast band brownish olive, lores greyish.

   WHITE-BROWED JUNGLE FLYCATCHER, *Rhinomyias gularis*. 6'' (15cm). From other jungle flycatchers by white eyebrow. Montane.

7. MAROON-BREASTED FLYCATCHER, *Philentoma velatum*. 7'' (18cm). Female lacks maroon on breast, but has black throat.

8. RUFOUS-WINGED FLYCATCHER, *Philentoma pyrhopterum*. 6'' (15cm). Blue replaced by pale brown in female. Some males are all blue.

9. MANGROVE WHISTLER, *Pachycephala cinerea*. 5½'' (14cm). Thick bill; greyish head; brown back; no rufous.

10. VELVET-FRONTED NUTHATCH, *Sitta frontalis*. 5'' (13cm).

PLATE XXXVIII

THREE INCHES

0   1   2   3

0   25   50   75

75mm

PLATE XXXIX
FLOWERPECKERS

1. SCARLET-BREASTED FLOWERPECKER, *Prionochilus thoracicus*. 3½'' (9cm). Female olive brown, with greyish throat, orange breast, and yellow rump.

2. YELLOW-RUMPED FLOWERPECKER, *Prionochilus xanthopygius*. 3½'' (9cm). Female like Scarlet-breasted female but greener with no orange on breast.

3. CRIMSON-BREASTED FLOWERPECKER, *Prionochilus percussus*. 3¾'' (9.5cm). Female like Yellow-breasted, but streaks indistinct.

4. YELLOW-BREASTED FLOWERPECKER, *Prionochilus maculatus*. 3½'' (9cm).

5. YELLOW-VENTED FLOWERPECKER, *Dicaeum chrysorrheum*. 3¾'' (9.5cm).

6. BROWN-BACKED FLOWERPECKER, *Dicaeum everetti*. 4'' (10cm).

7. PLAIN FLOWERPECKER, *Dicaeum concolor*. 2¾'' (7cm). Thinner bill than Brown-backed Flowerpecker.

8. BLACK-SIDED FLOWERPECKER, *Dicaeum celebicum*. 3'' (7.5cm). Female like Plain Flowerpecker, but larger. Montane.

9. SCARLET-BACKED FLOWERPECKER, *Dicaeum cruentatum*. 3'' (7.5cm). Female greyish with scarlet rump.

10. SCARLET-HEADED FLOWERPECKER, *Dicaeum trochileum*. 3'' (7.5cm). Female like Scarlet-backed female, but washed with red on mantle and head. S. Borneo only.

11. ORANGE-BELLIED FLOWERPECKER, *Dicaeum trigonostigma*. 3'' (7.5cm). Female duller, blue replaced by olive.

PLATE XXXIX

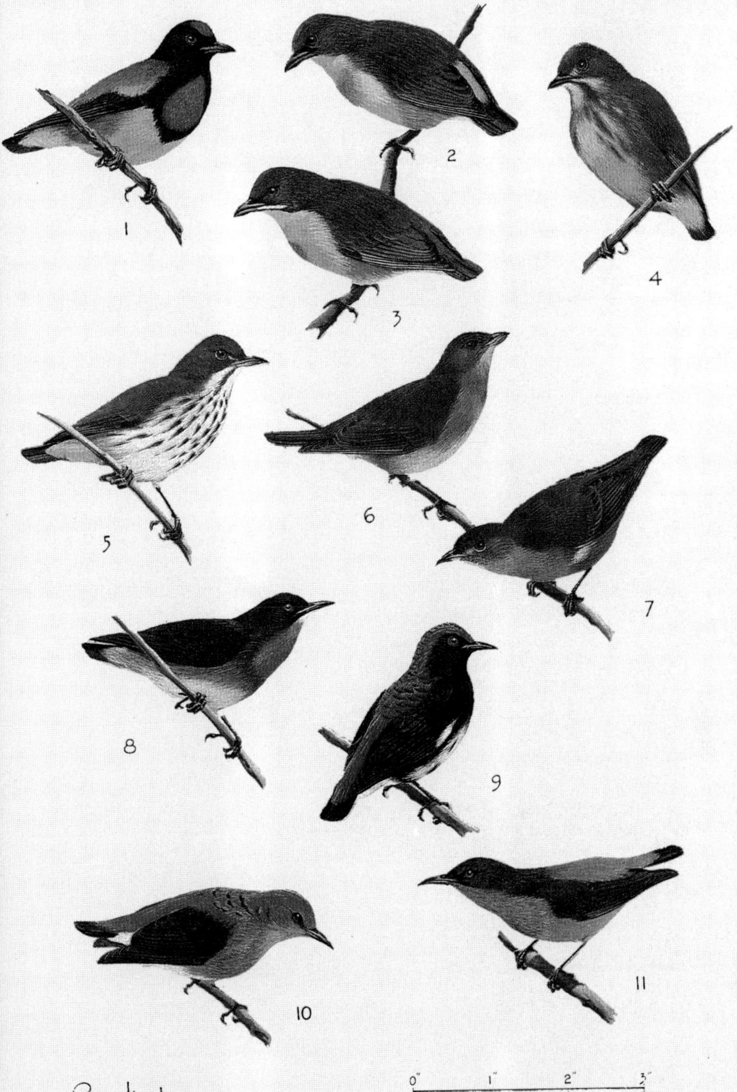

AnnHughes
1959

0"   1"   2"   3"
0   25   mm   50   75

PLATE XL
SUNBIRDS

1. PLAIN SUNBIRD, *Anthreptes simplex*. 5" (13cm). Female lacks green forehead.

2. BROWN-THROATED SUNBIRD, *Anthreptes malacensis*. a) Male, b) Female. 5" (13cm). Female: bright yellow underparts.

3. RED-THROATED SUNBIRD, *Anthreptes rhodolaema*. 5" (13cm). From Brown-throated Sunbird male by redder wing coverts; greener belly. Female like Brown-throated Sunbird female, but belly more olive.

4. RUBY-CHEEKED SUNBIRD, *Anthreptes singalensis*. 4½" (11cm). Female dull olive above; yellow below except pale red throat.

5. PURPLE-NAPED SUNBIRD, *Hypogramma hypogrammicum*. 5½" (14cm). Female lacks purple nape and rump.

6. PURPLE-THROATED SUNBIRD, *Nectarinia sperata*. 3½" (9cm). Female like Crimson Sunbird female, but tail shorter and blacker.

7. COPPER-THROATED SUNBIRD, *Nectarinia calcostetha*. 5" (13cm). Female like Crimson Sunbird female, but larger; greyish head; white tips to black tail.

8. YELLOW-BREASTED (OLIVE-BACKED) SUNBIRD, *Nectarinia jugularis*. a) Male, b) Female. 4" (10cm). Female from Brown-throated Sunbird female by white tail tips; more curved black bill.

9. CRIMSON SUNBIRD, *Aethopyga siparaja*. a) Male, b) Female. 4" (10cm).

10. SCARLET SUNBIRD, *Aethopyga mystacalis*. 4½" (11cm). Female like Crimson Sunbird female, but wings and tail washed with red.

PLATE XL

THREE INCHES

0   1   2   3

0   25   50   75

75mm

PLATE XLI
SPIDERHUNTERS

1. LITTLE SPIDERHUNTER, *Arachnothera longirostra*. 6'' (15cm).

2. THICK-BILLED SPIDERHUNTER, *Arachnothera crassirostris*. 6'' (15cm). From Little Spiderhunter by yellow chin, darker plumage.

3. SPECTACLED SPIDERHUNTER, *Arachnothera flavigaster*. 7'' (18cm). Small yellow ear patch, broad yellow eyering.

4. LONG-BILLED SPIDERHUNTER, *Arachnothera robusta*. 7½'' (19cm).

5. YELLOW-EARED SPIDERHUNTER, *Arachnothera chrysogenys*. 6½'' (16cm). Large yellow ear patch, narrow yellow eyering.

6. GREY-BREASTED SPIDERHUNTER, *Arachnothera affinis*. 6½'' (16cm).

7.* WHITEHEAD'S SPIDERHUNTER, *Arachnothera juliae*. 7'' (18cm). Montane.

PLATE XLI

THREE INCHES

0   1   2   3

0   25   50   75

75 mm

PLATE XLII
WHITE-EYES, MUNIAS and Buntings

1. ORIENTAL WHITE-EYE, *Zosterops palpebrosa.* 3¾'' (9cm). Coastal.

2. EVERETT'S WHITE-EYE, *Zosterops everetti.* 3¾'' (9cm). From Oriental by broader yellow ventral line; darker grey flanks. Interior.

3. BLACK-CAPPED WHITE-EYE, *Zosterops atricapilla.* 3¾'' (9cm).

4. JAVAN WHITE-EYE, *Zosterops flava.* 3¾'' (9cm). No black loral spot; tail < 33mm. Rare.

5. MANGROVE WHITE-EYE, *Zosterops chloris.* 4'' (10cm). Black loral spot; tail 35-40mm. Karamata Island only.

6. LONG-TAILED MUNIA (PIN-TAILED PARROTFINCH), *Erythrura prasina.* 4½'' (11mm). Male tail 1'' (2.5cm) longer.

7. BAMBOO MUNIA (TAWNY-BREASTED PARROTFINCH), *Erythrura hyperythra.* 4'' (10cm).

8. JAVA SPARROW, *Padda oryzivora.* 6'' (15cm). Introduced.

9.* DUSKY MUNIA, *Lonchura fuscans.* 4'' (10cm).

10. WHITE-BELLIED MUNIA, *Lonchura leucogastra.* 4½'' (11cm).

11. CHESTNUT MUNIA, *Lonchura malacca.* 4½'' (11cm). Immature is all rufous.

RED AVADAVAT, *Amandava amandava.* 4'' (10cm). Male red with white spots. Female brown with white spots and red rump. Bill red. Introduced.

✓ (EURASIAN) TREE SPARROW, *Passer montanus.* 5½'' (14cm). Brown streaked back; whitish belly; chestnut brown cap; black bib; white cheek with black spot.

LITTLE BUNTING, *Emberiza pusilla.* 5½'' (14cm). Brown upperparts with black streaks; whitish finely streaked underparts; rufous crown stripe and cheeks. Vagrant.

YELLOW-BREASTED BUNTING, *Emberiza aureola.* 6½'' (16cm). Conspicuous white wing patches; white outer tail feathers. Male: chestnut back and breast band; yellow breast and belly. Female: brown with buffy streaked underparts; buffy eyebrow. Vagrant.

PLATE XLII

Ann Hughes
1958

THREE INCHES

PLATE XLIII
DRONGOS AND ORIOLES

1. CROW-BILLED DRONGO, *Dicrurus annectans.* 10'' (25cm). Deeply forked tail. Migrant.

2. GREY (ASHY) DRONGO, *Dicrurus leucophaeus.* 10'' (25cm).

3. GREATER RACKET-TAILED DRONGO, *Dicrurus paradiseus.* 10'' (25cm) tail up to 12'' (30cm) extra. Rackets sometimes missing: from Crow-billed Drongo by less forked tail.

4. SPANGLED DRONGO, *Dicrurus hottentottus.* 10'' (25cm). Mainly montane.

5. BRONZED DRONGO, *Dicrurus aeneus.* 8'' (20cm).

6. * BLACK ORIOLE, *Oriolus hosei.* 8½'' (22cm).

7. BLACK-HOODED ORIOLE, *Oriolus xanthornus.* 9'' (23cm). Immature has white throat streaked with black; yellow streaks on forehead.

8. BLACK-NAPED ORIOLE, *Oriolus chinensis.* 9'' (23cm). Immature streaked underneath. Rare.

9. BLACK-AND-CRIMSON ORIOLE, *Oriolus cruentus.* 8½'' (22cm). Montane.

10. DARK-THROATED ORIOLE, *Oriolus xanthonotus.* a) Male, b) Female.

PLATE XLIII

Aw Hughes
1958

PLATE XLIV
STARLINGS, PIES AND CROWS

1. PHILIPPINE GLOSSY STARLING, *Aplonis panayensis*. 8" (20cm) a) Adult; b) Immature.

2. VIOLET-BACKED STARLING, *Sturnus philippensis*. 6½" (16cm) a) Male; b) Female. Migrant.

   DAURIAN (PURPLE-BACKED) STARLING, *Sturnus sturninus*. 7" (18cm). Similar to Violet-backed but no chestnut on neck; purple nape; plain white underparts. Vagrant.

   CHINESE (WHITE-SHOULDERED) STARLING, *Sturnus sinensis*. 9" (22cm). Pale grey with broad white shoulder patch on black wings; white or buff-tipped black tail. Vagrant.

   COMMON MYNA, *Acridotheres tristis*. 10" (25cm). Brown body; black head; yellow bill and facial skin; white patch in wing. Introduced.

   CRESTED MYNA, *Acridotheres cristatellus*. 10½" (27cm). Black with short crest; ivory yellow bill; white patch in wing; undertail coverts black with white scales. Introduced.

3. GRACKLE or HILL MYNA, *Gracula religiosa*. 12" (30cm).

4. SHORT-TAILED GREEN MAGPIE, *Cissa thalassina*. 12" (30cm). Montane.

5. COMMON GREEN MAGPIE, *Cissa chinensis*. 13" (33cm). Submontane.

6. CRESTED JAY, *Platylophus galericulatus*. 10" (25cm).

7. MALAYSIAN TREEPIE, *Dendrocitta occipitalis*. 17" (43cm). Montane.

   RACKET-TAILED TREEPIE, *Crypsirina temia*. 13" (33cm). Black with long spatulate tail. Rare.

8. BLACK MAGPIE, *Platysmurus leucopterus*. 14" (36cm).

9. SLENDER-BILLED CROW, *Corvus enca*. 18" (46cm). Thinner bill; higher pitched rather varied call.

10. JUNGLE (LARGE-BILLED) CROW, *Corvus macrorhynchos*. 20" (50cm). Heavy bill; call a deep-throated 'caw'. Rare.

PLATE XLIV

Hughes
1958

PLATE XLV
SOME RARE BIRDS OF BORNEO

1. MALAYSIAN HONEYGUIDE, *Indicator archipelagicus.* 6½'' (17cm).

2. GREAT TIT, *Parus major.* 5'' (13cm).

3. * BORNEAN BRISTLEHEAD, *Pityriasis gymnocephala.* 10'' (25cm).

4. SIBERIAN THRUSH. *Zoothera sibirica.* 9'' (23cm). Female brown with barred breast; buffy eyebrow; white stripe under wing. Vagrant.

5. ORANGE-HEADED THRUSH, *Zoothera citrina.* 8'' (20cm).

6. CHESTNUT-CAPPED THRUSH, *Zoothera interpres.* 6'' (15cm).

7. BLACK-BROWED BABBLER, *Trichastoma perspicillatum.* 6'' (15cm).

8.* EVERETT'S THRUSH, *Zoothera everetti.* 8'' (20cm).

PLATE **XLV**

1

2

3

4

5

6

7

8

0"   3"   6"
0   50   mm   100   150

1958

INDEX TO COMMON NAMES

INDEX TO GENERA

122